THE GLOSSARY OF
AGILE
MANAGEMENT

Compiled & Edited By:
Sachin Pasayat

Rhythm

Independent
Publication

THE GLOSSARY OF AGILE MANAGEMENT

Compiled & Edited By:
Sachin Pasayat

ISBN:9798861157711

9798861157711

Published by:
Rhythm Independent Publication,
Jinkethimmanahalli, Varanasi, Bengaluru, Karnataka, India - 560036

For all types of correspondence, send your mails to the provided address above.

The information presented herein has been collated from a diverse range of sources, comprehensive perspective on the subject matter.

Agile Process/ Project Management

The Agile Process is a project management methodology that emphasizes flexibility, collaboration, and iterative development. It is based on the principles outlined in the Agile Manifesto, which values individuals and interactions, working software, customer collaboration, and responding to change.

Agile Project Management is an approach to managing projects that focuses on delivering value to customers through early and continuous delivery of software. It prioritizes adaptability and responsiveness to changing requirements and customer needs. The Agile Project Management discipline includes several frameworks, such as Scrum, Kanban, and Lean, which provide specific guidelines and practices for managing projects in an Agile manner.

Acceptance Criteria

Acceptance Criteria in the context of Agile Process and Project Management disciplines refers to a set of conditions or requirements that define when a user story or a product feature is considered complete and satisfied. These criteria are used to determine if the work done by the development team meets the expectations of the stakeholders, customers, or end-users.

Acceptance Criteria provide specific details and guidelines for the development team on what needs to be produced and achieved in order for a user story or feature to be deemed successful and ready for release. They help in aligning the understanding of the desired outcome between the development team and the stakeholders.

Adaptability

Adaptability in the context of Agile Process and Project Management disciplines refers to the ability of a team, project, or process to respond and adjust to changes in a flexible and efficient manner. It is the capacity to embrace uncertainty, handle unforeseen challenges, and quickly adapt strategies or plans to ensure project success.

Agile methodologies, such as Scrum or Kanban, are based on the principle of adaptability. They recognize that change is inevitable and prioritize the ability to respond to it effectively. By embracing iterative and incremental development, Agile teams can continuously gather feedback and adapt their approach accordingly. This allows them to stay on track, minimize risk, and deliver valuable outcomes.

Adaptive Leadership

Adaptive leadership within the context of Agile Process and Project Management disciplines refers to the ability of leaders to navigate and respond to the evolving and complex nature of projects and processes in an agile and flexible manner.

Adaptive leadership involves being responsive to change and uncertainty, constantly adjusting plans and strategies to meet emerging needs and conditions. It goes beyond traditional hierarchical decision-making by empowering teams to collaborate and take ownership of their work. Adaptive leaders create an environment where innovation can thrive, encouraging experimentation and learning from failures.

Adaptive Planning

Adaptive planning, in the context of Agile Process and Project Management disciplines, refers to a flexible and iterative approach to planning and managing projects. It emphasizes the ability to respond and adapt to changes throughout the project lifecycle, rather than adhering strictly to a pre-defined plan.

Agile project management methodologies, such as Scrum or Kanban, embrace adaptive planning as a core principle. Instead of creating a detailed, long-term plan at the beginning of the project, adaptive planning involves breaking the project down into smaller, manageable increments called iterations or sprints.

During each iteration, the project team collaboratively determines the work to be done, typically prioritized by value or importance, and assigns it to team members. This enables the team to quickly respond to changing priorities, new requirements, or unforeseen challenges as they arise.

Adaptive planning also encourages continuous learning and improvement through regular project retrospectives and feedback loops. These feedback loops allow the team to reflect on their progress, learn from their experiences, and make necessary adjustments to their approach for future iterations.

By embracing adaptive planning, Agile project teams are better equipped to navigate uncertainties and manage changing priorities. They are able to deliver incremental value to stakeholders more frequently, adapt to new information or customer feedback, and ultimately increase the chances of project success.

Adaptive Process

The adaptive process is a fundamental concept in Agile Process and Project Management disciplines. It refers to the ability to adapt the project management approach and processes based on the changing needs and requirements of the project. Unlike traditional project management methods, which follow a rigid and predefined plan, the adaptive process embraces change and welcomes new insights throughout the project lifecycle.

Agile methodologies such as Scrum, Kanban, and Lean rely on the adaptive process to deliver valuable products efficiently. The adaptive process involves continuous planning, monitoring, and adjusting to ensure that the project stays on track and delivers the expected outcomes. It empowers the project team to respond promptly to changes, risks, and issues, enabling them to make informed decisions and take appropriate actions.

Agile Adoption

Agile adoption refers to the implementation and integration of Agile principles and practices within the context of the Agile Process and Project Management disciplines. It is the process of introducing and institutionalizing Agile methodologies, such as Scrum or Kanban, in an organization to improve the efficiency, effectiveness, and adaptability of project management processes.

Agile adoption involves a mindset shift from traditional, linear project management approaches to an iterative and collaborative approach. It focuses on delivering customer value early and frequently through short development cycles called sprints or iterations. This allows for continuous feedback and adjustment, ensuring that the project stays aligned with customer needs and business goals.

During Agile adoption, cross-functional teams are formed, consisting of various stakeholders, including developers, testers, business analysts, and customers. These teams self-organize and collaborate to plan, execute, and deliver projects incrementally. Daily stand-up meetings, sprint planning, backlog grooming, and retrospectives are common Agile practices used during the adoption process.

Agile adoption also emphasizes open and transparent communication, fostering a culture of collaboration and trust between team members and stakeholders. It encourages adaptive planning, embracing change throughout the project lifecycle, and incorporating feedback from customers and end-users. This iterative approach allows for flexibility, faster response to market or customer changes, and early identification of potential risks or issues.

2

In summary, Agile adoption is the process of implementing Agile methodologies and practices within the Agile Process and Project Management disciplines. It enables organizations to improve project outcomes, increase customer satisfaction, and enhance team collaboration and communication.

Agile Architecture

Agile Architecture refers to the practice of incorporating architectural principles and design decisions into the Agile Process and Project Management disciplines. It involves the continuous collaboration between architects, developers, and stakeholders to create a flexible and adaptable architectural framework.

In an Agile environment, the focus is on delivering high-value working software in short iterations. Agile Architecture supports this by providing a foundation that allows for easy adaptability and change. It embraces the principles of the Agile Manifesto, such as individuals and interactions over processes and tools, and responding to change over following a plan.

Agile Architecture promotes the concept of evolutionary design, where the architecture evolves gradually throughout the development process. It emphasizes simplicity, modularity, and maintaining a balance between short-term functionality and long-term sustainability.

The key elements of Agile Architecture include continuous architectural refactoring, which involves making incremental changes to improve the quality, maintainability, and extensibility of the architecture. It also involves the use of architectural patterns and principles to guide the development process and ensure consistency and coherence.

Furthermore, Agile Architecture encourages the use of cross-functional teams, where architects and developers work closely together to make architectural decisions. It promotes open communication, collaboration, and knowledge sharing to create a shared understanding of the architecture and facilitate informed decision-making.

Overall, Agile Architecture recognizes the importance of balancing agility with architectural integrity. It enables organizations to respond to changing requirements and market conditions while maintaining a solid architectural foundation for long-term success.

Agile Artifacts

Agile artifacts refer to the tangible and visible documents, deliverables, and materials that are created and used during an Agile project. These artifacts serve as communication tools and provide transparency, traceability, and the necessary information for decision-making throughout the project lifecycle. They are maintained and updated regularly, capturing the evolving project requirements and progress.

The main Agile artifacts include the product backlog, sprint backlog, user stories, task boards, burn-down charts, and release plans. The product backlog is a prioritized list of user requirements or features, known as user stories. It outlines the project scope and serves as a single source of truth for the development team. The sprint backlog is a subset of the product backlog, containing the user stories and tasks selected for a specific sprint or iteration.

User stories are concise descriptions of functionality or features from the user's perspective and serve as the building blocks for development. Task boards, often visualized as Kanban boards or Scrum boards, provide visibility into the progress of individual tasks and the sprint as a whole. Burn-down charts represent the remaining work throughout a sprint, helping teams stay on track and manage their time effectively.

Release plans outline the high-level timeline and delivery schedule for product releases. They provide a framework for coordinating development efforts and managing stakeholder expectations. Throughout the Agile project, these artifacts are used collaboratively by the development team, product owner, and scrum master to ensure shared understanding and facilitate decision-making.

Agile Assessment

3

An Agile Assessment is a systematic evaluation of Agile processes and project management practices to determine their effectiveness and identify areas for improvement. It is conducted to ensure that the Agile principles and values are being followed and to drive continuous improvement in the Agile implementation.

The Agile Assessment aims to assess the project's adherence to Agile principles, as outlined in the Agile Manifesto, and evaluate how well the Agile methodologies are being adopted. It focuses on evaluating the effectiveness of Agile practices such as iterative development, frequent feedback, collaboration, and flexibility in responding to changing requirements.

The Agile Assessment process typically involves reviewing project documentation, conducting interviews with project team members, and observing Agile ceremonies such as sprint planning, daily stand-ups, and sprint reviews. The assessment may also involve gathering feedback from stakeholders to assess their satisfaction and involvement in the project.

The key objectives of an Agile Assessment are to identify strengths and weaknesses in the Agile implementation, assess the maturity level of Agile practices, and recommend improvements to optimize project delivery. It helps teams and organizations to identify areas where Agile methodologies can be enhanced, such as refining the backlog management process, improving communication and collaboration within the team, or enhancing the feedback loop with stakeholders.

Agile Backlog

Agile Backlog The Agile Backlog is a fundamental component of the Agile process and project management disciplines. It serves as a dynamic and prioritized list of requirements, enhancements, and tasks that need to be completed to deliver a successful product or project. In Agile, the backlog is not a static document but rather a living artifact that evolves and adapts throughout the project lifecycle. It captures the collective understanding of the team's vision, goals, and objectives, and provides a transparent and visible overview of the work to be done. The backlog is typically owned by the Product Owner, who is responsible for constantly refining and reprioritizing it based on customer feedback, changing business priorities, and emerging market trends. Items in the backlog are expressed as user stories, which are concise and specific statements that describe a desired functionality, feature, or user interaction. These user stories are typically written from the perspective of the end-user and are refined over time through collaboration and feedback from the development team. One of the key attributes of the Agile backlog is its prioritization. Items are ordered based on their value to the customer and end-user, with the most valuable items placed at the top. This allows the team to focus on delivering incremental value early in the project and ensures that the highest priority items are always considered for implementation. Additionally, the Agile backlog is flexible and adaptable to change. As new insights are gained, priorities shift, or market conditions change, items in the backlog can be reprioritized or even removed. This allows the team to respond to new information and adapt to evolving requirements, resulting in a more customer-centric and value-driven approach to project management. In summary, the Agile backlog is a dynamic and prioritized list of requirements and tasks that evolves throughout the project. It captures the team's vision and goals, supports collaboration and transparency, and enables a customer-focused and adaptable approach to project delivery.

Agile Ceremonies

Agile Ceremonies are a set of recurring events or meetings that take place throughout an Agile project to facilitate effective communication, collaboration, and decision-making among team members. These ceremonies provide opportunities for the team to reflect on their progress, plan for the future, and address any obstacles or issues that may arise during the project. The most commonly used Agile ceremonies include:

1. Sprint Planning: This ceremony occurs at the beginning of each sprint and involves the entire team discussing and agreeing upon the scope of work to be completed during the upcoming sprint. The team creates a sprint backlog and identifies the tasks needed to achieve the sprint goals. 2. Daily Stand-up: Also known as the daily scrum, this short and focused meeting takes place every day to provide team members with a forum for sharing their progress, challenges,

and plans for the day. It promotes transparency and enables the team to identify and address any obstacles. 3. Sprint Review: At the end of each sprint, the team demonstrates their completed work to stakeholders and collects feedback. This ceremony encourages collaboration and validates the team's accomplishments, providing an opportunity to adjust priorities and refine the product backlog if necessary. 4. Sprint Retrospective: Following the sprint review, the team reflects on their performance and identifies areas for improvement. They discuss what went well, what didn't go well, and brainstorm potential solutions to enhance their processes and practices. These Agile ceremonies ensure that the team remains aligned, maintains a shared understanding of the project goals, and continuously improves their work. By following these recurring events, Agile teams can foster collaboration, adaptability, and deliver value to the customer in an iterative and incremental manner.

Agile Coach

An Agile Coach is a role within the Agile Process and Project Management disciplines that focuses on guiding and supporting teams as they adopt and implement Agile practices. The primary responsibility of an Agile Coach is to help teams improve their overall effectiveness and productivity by facilitating the use of Agile principles and frameworks.

The Agile Coach acts as a mentor and advisor to the team, providing guidance on how to best apply Agile methods to their specific project or initiative. They help the team to understand and embrace Agile values and principles, and assist in the adoption of Agile practices such as Scrum, Kanban, or Lean. The Agile Coach also works with stakeholders and management to ensure alignment with Agile principles and to remove any barriers or impediments to success.

As a facilitator, the Agile Coach helps to create an environment that is conducive to collaboration, communication, and continuous improvement. They guide the team in self-organizing and becoming more autonomous, and foster a culture of learning and experimentation. The Agile Coach also helps to identify and resolve any conflicts or obstacles that may arise during the Agile implementation process.

Overall, the Agile Coach serves as a catalyst for change and supports teams in their journey to becoming more Agile. They provide guidance, support, and expertise to help teams successfully embrace and implement Agile practices, ultimately leading to more effective and efficient project delivery.

Agile Coaching

Agile Coaching is a discipline within Agile Process and Project Management that focuses on guiding and supporting teams in their adoption and implementation of Agile principles and practices. Agile Coaching aims to facilitate the Agile mindset and promote collaboration, self-organization, and continuous improvement within Agile teams.

An Agile Coach typically works closely with project teams, providing guidance, mentoring, and training to help them navigate the complexities of Agile methodologies. They help teams understand and apply Agile principles and frameworks, such as Scrum or Kanban, and support them in achieving their project goals and delivering value to their stakeholders.

The primary role of an Agile Coach is to foster a culture of learning and adaptation, enabling teams to embrace change and respond effectively to evolving requirements and market dynamics. They help teams improve their Agile practices, resolve conflicts, and enhance communication and collaboration among team members and stakeholders.

Agile Coaching involves various activities, including facilitating Agile ceremonies, such as daily stand-ups, sprint planning, and retrospectives, and coaching individuals and teams on Agile techniques and tools. Coaches also assist in identifying and addressing impediments that hinder team progress, and work collaboratively with team members to find creative solutions.

In summary, Agile Coaching plays a crucial role in supporting Agile teams and organizations in their journey towards agility, by providing guidance, support, and enabling continuous learning and improvement. It helps teams embrace Agile values and principles, adapt to changing circumstances, and consistently deliver value to their customers.

Agile Contract

Agile Contract is a formal agreement between a customer and a supplier in the context of Agile Process and Project Management disciplines. It outlines the terms and conditions for the delivery of a project using Agile methodologies. In the Agile approach, flexibility and adaptability are key principles. The Agile Contract reflects this by being more flexible compared to traditional fixed-price contracts. It acknowledges that requirements and priorities may change throughout the project, allowing for continuous collaboration and feedback. Instead of specifying all requirements upfront, the Agile Contract focuses on high-level objectives and goals. It allows for iterative development and delivery, with frequent opportunities for the customer to review and provide feedback on the work completed so far. The Agile Contract also includes provisions for scope changes, which are expected in Agile projects. It sets out a process for managing changes to the project's scope, ensuring that both parties are aligned on the impact and cost of any changes. Furthermore, the Agile Contract emphasizes regular communication and collaboration between the customer and the supplier. It promotes transparency, trust, and shared responsibility for the project's success. The contract may include provisions for daily stand-up meetings, review sessions, and retrospective meetings to facilitate continuous improvement. Overall, an Agile Contract is a dynamic and flexible agreement that enables the customer and supplier to work together effectively in an Agile project, allowing for adaptation and continuous value delivery based on evolving requirements and customer feedback.

Agile Contracts

Agile Contracts refer to an approach of legal agreements that are aligned with the principles and values of Agile Process and Project Management. In this context, an Agile Contract is characterized by its flexibility, adaptability, and collaboration-focused nature.

Unlike traditional contracts that are rigid and focused on detailed specifications, Agile Contracts prioritize the ability to respond to change and embrace uncertainty. They emphasize open communication, frequent collaboration, and shared responsibility between the parties involved.

Agile Development

Agile Development is a framework and iterative approach to software development that emphasizes flexibility, collaboration, and incremental delivery. It is characterized by short development cycles, referred to as sprints, where requirements and solutions evolve through the collaborative effort of cross-functional teams. Agile aims to deliver high-quality software quickly, by promoting adaptive planning, evolutionary development, early and continuous delivery, and constant improvement.

In the Agile process, the development team works closely with the customer or product owner to continuously refine and prioritize the requirements, enabling the team to deliver functioning software at the end of each sprint. The team is self-organizing and cross-functional, which means they have the ability to make decisions and take ownership, leveraging their diverse skills and knowledge to produce the best possible outcomes.

Agile project management is a fundamental aspect of Agile Development, ensuring alignment between the development team, stakeholders, and the organization. It involves breaking down initiatives, known as epics, into smaller user stories that can be prioritized and scheduled in the sprint backlog. This provides a transparent and collaborative approach to project planning, allowing for frequent inspections and adaptations throughout the development process.

Overall, Agile Development promotes customer satisfaction, collaboration, and adaptability within software development projects. It focuses on delivering incremental value to customers through regular and frequent releases, allowing for continuous feedback and improvement. By embracing change and responding to evolving requirements, Agile Development enables teams to deliver high-quality software that meets customer needs in an efficient and timely manner.

Agile Engineering

Agile Engineering is an approach within the Agile Process and Project Management disciplines that emphasizes continuous development, delivery, and improvement. It focuses on collaboration and flexibility to meet changing requirements and customer needs.

In Agile Engineering, cross-functional teams work together in short iterations, known as sprints, to deliver incremental solutions. These teams are self-organized and empowered to make decisions, ensuring quick feedback and minimizing delays, as well as enabling faster delivery of value to the customer.

The Agile Engineering approach embraces frequent testing and integration to validate and improve the quality of the software being developed. Through continuous integration, teams can catch and address issues early, avoiding major disruptions and reducing rework. This iterative process also allows for continuous learning and refinement of the project scope and requirements.

Agile Engineering promotes the use of automated testing tools and frameworks to streamline the testing process and increase efficiency. By automating repetitive tasks, such as unit testing and regression testing, teams can save time and focus on delivering high-value features.

The Agile Engineering approach recognizes the importance of feedback loops with customers and stakeholders. Regular feedback and collaboration ensure that the delivered software meets their expectations and aligns with their evolving needs, reducing the risk of developing unwanted or unnecessary features.

Agile Estimating And Planning

Agile Estimating and Planning is a vital component of the Agile Process and Project Management disciplines. It entails the process of determining the effort, time, and resources required to complete a project within an Agile methodology.

In Agile Project Management, estimation and planning are iterative and collaborative processes. The objective is to create a realistic and achievable project plan by breaking down the work into smaller, more manageable tasks and estimating the effort required for each task. This approach enables the team to adapt and respond to changes more effectively, resulting in improved project outcomes.

The estimation process in Agile involves the participation of the entire project team, including the Product Owner, Scrum Master, and development team members. It is based on relative sizing or story points, rather than traditional time-based estimates. The team collaborates to assign story points to each task or user story based on its complexity, effort, and dependencies. These story points represent the effort required to complete a task relative to other tasks.

Agile Planning focuses on creating a flexible and adaptable project plan that can accommodate changes and uncertainties. It involves prioritizing tasks based on their business value and dependencies, establishing a sprint backlog, and defining the scope for each sprint. The team continuously re-evaluates and adjusts the plan as they gain more understanding and insights throughout the project's lifecycle.

Agile Estimation

Agile Estimation is a fundamental aspect of the Agile Process and Project Management disciplines. It refers to the practice of estimating the effort, time, and resources required to complete a project or deliver a specific feature or functionality within an Agile environment.

Unlike traditional project management approaches that rely on detailed upfront planning and documentation, Agile Estimation takes a more iterative and collaborative approach. It is based on the principles of Agile, which emphasize adaptability, flexibility, and continuous improvement.

Agile Estimation involves breaking down the project or feature into smaller, more manageable tasks or user stories. These tasks are then estimated by the Agile team using various techniques, such as story points, planning poker, or t-shirt sizes. The estimations are typically done in relative terms, considering the complexity, uncertainty, and dependencies of each task.

The Agile Estimation process encourages active involvement and collaboration among all stakeholders, including the product owner, development team, and other relevant parties. It promotes open discussions, shared understanding, and transparency, allowing for more accurate and realistic estimations.

The main goal of Agile Estimation is to provide the team with a clear understanding of the work required and enable them to make informed decisions regarding priorities, planning, and resource allocation. It also helps in identifying potential risks, bottlenecks, or dependencies that may impact the project's success.

Agile Facilitation

Agile facilitation refers to the practice of guiding and enabling a team to effectively and efficiently collaborate and iterate throughout the Agile process and project management disciplines. It involves creating an environment that fosters open communication, collaboration, and learning, ultimately leading to the successful delivery of high-quality products or services.

An agile facilitator plays a crucial role in helping teams embrace and implement Agile principles and practices. They are responsible for facilitating team meetings, such as daily stand-ups, sprint planning, retrospectives, and demos, ensuring that the sessions are productive and focused on achieving the project's goals and objectives.

The primary objective of agile facilitation is to remove any impediments or barriers that hinder the team's progress and inhibits their ability to deliver value to the customer. The facilitator acts as a neutral guide, helping the team to identify and address any issues, conflicts, or challenges that arise during the project's lifecycle.

Agile facilitation also involves empowering the team to self-organize and make informed decisions. The facilitator encourages collaboration and knowledge sharing, fostering a culture of continuous improvement and learning. They may use various techniques, such as visual aids, brainstorming, and collaborative games, to enhance team engagement and creativity.

By embracing the agile facilitation approach, teams can streamline their processes, improve transparency, and increase their productivity. The facilitator serves as a catalyst for effective collaboration and empowers the team to take ownership of the project, resulting in the timely delivery of high-quality products or services that meet the customer's expectations.

Agile Fluency

Agile Fluency refers to the level of proficiency and effectiveness that a team or organization has achieved in implementing Agile practices in both the Agile Process and Project Management disciplines. It represents the team's ability to deliver quality products in a timely and predictable manner while continuously adapting to changing requirements and customer needs.

At its core, Agile Fluency is about embracing the Agile mindset and values, such as collaboration, transparency, and iterative development. It involves utilizing Agile principles and practices, such as Scrum or Kanban, to enable teams to work together effectively, communicate efficiently, and deliver value to customers incrementally. This includes practices like daily stand-ups, backlog grooming, and frequent retrospectives to continuously improve the team's performance and productivity.

Agile Fluency is typically measured along a continuum of four stages: focusing on individual skills, delivering value as a team, optimizing team performance, and finally becoming a true Agile organization. Each stage represents a different level of proficiency and ability to apply Agile principles to drive better outcomes.

Ultimately, Agile Fluency is not just about following Agile rituals and processes, but rather about fostering a culture of collaboration, learning, and improvement. It requires a deep commitment from the team and organization to embrace Agile values and continuously strive for excellence in delivering customer value through iterative and incremental development.

Agile Framework

The Agile Framework is an iterative and incremental approach to project management and software development. It is based on the principles outlined in the Agile Manifesto and seeks to prioritize delivering working software that meets customer needs over comprehensive documentation.

In the Agile Framework, projects are divided into short iterations, typically lasting two to four weeks, called sprints. Each sprint focuses on delivering a small piece of working functionality. This allows for regular feedback from stakeholders and the ability to adapt and change based on that feedback.

Agile emphasizes collaboration and communication within cross-functional teams, which include members from different disciplines such as development, testing, and product management. These teams work closely together throughout the entire project, ensuring a high level of transparency and efficiency.

The Agile Framework encourages continuous integration and continuous delivery, where software is regularly tested, integrated, and deployed. This provides stakeholders with frequent updates and allows for constant improvement and learning.

One of the key principles of the Agile Framework is the ability to respond to change. This means that requirements can evolve throughout the project, and adjustments can be made accordingly. Agile also promotes self-organizing teams, empowering individuals to make decisions and take ownership.

In summary, the Agile Framework is a flexible and collaborative approach to project management and software development. It prioritizes delivering working software and encourages frequent feedback and adaptation to meet customer needs. By embracing change and empowering teams, Agile enables organizations to deliver high-quality products in a timely manner.

Agile Governance

Agile governance refers to the set of policies, practices, and processes that are implemented within an Agile project management framework to ensure efficient and effective decision-making, risk management, and overall project success.

In the context of Agile process and project management disciplines, governance is vital as it provides a structured approach to decision-making, enabling organizations to align project objectives with business goals, monitor progress, and mitigate risks in an Agile environment. Agile governance frameworks typically emphasize flexibility, adaptability, and collaborative decision-making to empower teams and individuals involved in the project.

Agile Leadership

Agile Leadership is a management approach that embraces the principles and values of the Agile Process and Project Management disciplines. It involves fostering a collaborative and flexible environment where teams are empowered to self-organize and make decisions based on feedback and information at hand.

Agile Leadership focuses on creating a shared vision, building trust, and promoting open communication within the team. It encourages individuals to take ownership of their responsibilities and encourages them to continuously improve their skills and knowledge. Agile Leaders prioritize the growth and development of their team members, fostering an environment of learning and adaptability.

Agile Manifesto

The Agile Manifesto is a formal declaration of four core values and twelve principles that guide the Agile process and project management disciplines. It was developed in 2001 by a group of software developers who were frustrated with traditional, rigid project management approaches.

The four core values of the Agile Manifesto are:

9

1. Individuals and interactions over processes and tools: This value emphasizes the importance of communication, collaboration, and teamwork. It recognizes that the success of a project depends on the people involved and their ability to work together effectively.

2. Working software over comprehensive documentation: This value emphasizes the importance of delivering working software that meets the needs of the stakeholders. It prioritizes the creation of tangible, functional products over excessive documentation and paperwork.

3. Customer collaboration over contract negotiation: This value emphasizes the importance of involving the customer throughout the development process. It encourages regular feedback and collaboration to ensure the end product aligns with the customer's needs and expectations.

4. Responding to change over following a plan: This value emphasizes the need for flexibility and adaptability in the face of changing requirements and circumstances. It recognizes that plans are not set in stone and that the ability to respond and adjust quickly is crucial to project success.

The twelve principles of the Agile Manifesto complement these core values and provide further guidance for Agile project management. They emphasize continuous delivery, sustainable development practices, self-organizing teams, regular reflection and adaptation, and close collaboration between the development team and stakeholders.

Agile Methodology

The Agile methodology is a project management approach that emphasizes flexibility, collaboration, and iterative development. It is based on the principles outlined in the Agile Manifesto, which values individuals and interactions, working software, customer collaboration, and responding to change.

Within the Agile methodology, projects are broken down into small, manageable tasks called user stories. These user stories are then prioritized and assigned to cross-functional teams, which include members from different disciplines such as development, testing, and design.

One of the key features of Agile is the use of sprints, which are short, time-boxed development cycles. During each sprint, the team works on a subset of user stories, delivering a potentially shippable product increment at the end. This allows for regular feedback and collaboration with stakeholders, ensuring that the project is on track and meeting customer needs.

Agile also promotes adaptive planning and continuous improvement. Project requirements and priorities can change throughout the development process, and the Agile methodology allows for flexibility and adjustments. This iterative approach enables the team to respond to feedback, identify and address issues early on, and deliver value to the customer more efficiently.

In summary, Agile is a project management methodology that prioritizes collaboration, flexibility, and iterative development. It allows teams to work in short, focused sprints, delivering incremental value and adapting to change throughout the project lifecycle.

Agile Metrics

Agile Metrics refer to the quantitative measures and indicators used in Agile Process and Project Management disciplines to assess the progress, performance, and health of Agile projects. These metrics help teams and organizations track and analyze key aspects of their Agile initiatives, enabling them to make data-driven decisions and continuously improve their processes.

Agile Metrics provide valuable insights into various aspects of project execution, allowing teams to monitor and adapt their approach to better meet customer needs and deliver value in a timely and efficient manner. They enable teams to track and evaluate important parameters such as velocity, lead time, cycle time, and burndown charts.

Velocity is a crucial Agile Metric that measures the amount of work completed by the team within a given time frame, providing an estimate of the team's capacity. It helps organizations plan and forecast project timelines and allocate resources effectively. Lead time measures the time taken from a customer's request to the delivery of the requested feature, enabling teams to identify bottlenecks and improve delivery speed. Cycle time measures the time taken from when work begins on a feature to when it is ready for delivery, helping teams identify areas for improvement in their development and testing practices.

Burndown charts depict the progress of work over time, showing the amount of work remaining and the projected completion date. They help teams to visualize their progress and make informed decisions regarding scope, priorities, and resource allocation. These metrics, along with other Agile Metrics, provide teams and stakeholders with objective data to assess performance, identify areas of improvement, and optimize their Agile processes for better outcomes.

Agile Mindset

The Agile Mindset is a fundamental philosophy and approach that is at the core of Agile Process and Project Management disciplines. It embodies a set of values and principles that guide individuals and teams in how they think and work towards the successful delivery of projects in an Agile environment.

An Agile Mindset encourages adaptability, collaboration, and iterative development. It emphasizes flexibility, responsiveness, and continuous learning. Agile practitioners embrace change and prioritize customer value, focusing on delivering working software incrementally, rather than following a rigid plan.

At its heart, the Agile Mindset values individuals and interactions over processes and tools. It promotes effective communication, trust, and empowerment within teams, acknowledging that people are the key drivers of successful project outcomes.

Furthermore, the Agile Mindset fosters a culture of transparency and shared responsibility. It encourages open feedback, regular reflection, and improvement. Agile practitioners value learning from both successes and failures, continuously evaluating and adapting their approaches to optimize value delivery.

In summary, the Agile Mindset is a foundational mindset that shapes the way individuals and teams approach Agile Process and Project Management. It embraces adaptability, collaboration, and continuous learning, focusing on delivering customer value through iterative development and embracing change.

Agile Modeling

Agile Modeling is a set of practices and principles that guide the modeling activities in the context of Agile Process and Project Management disciplines. It emphasizes the collaborative and iterative nature of modeling, aiming at creating simple yet effective models that communicate effectively.

In an Agile environment, modeling is seen as a tool for communication and understanding rather than as a comprehensive documentation effort. Agile Modeling recognizes that requirements and solutions evolve over time, and it adapts to changes by focusing on creating models that are just good enough for the current stage of the project.

The key principles of Agile Modeling include simplicity, flexibility, and active stakeholder participation. Models are kept simple to promote clarity and understanding, avoiding unnecessary complexity that can hinder communication. Flexibility is essential to accommodate changes, and models are updated and refined as new information becomes available or requirements change.

Active stakeholder participation is encouraged throughout the modeling process. Stakeholders are invited to provide feedback and validate models, ensuring that they accurately represent their needs and expectations. This collaborative approach fosters understanding and alignment among team members and stakeholders.

11

Agile Modeling promotes visual modeling techniques, such as diagrams and sketches, to enhance communication and facilitate understanding. These visual representations provide a shared language that allows team members to discuss and validate assumptions, clarify requirements, and visualize potential solutions.

In summary, Agile Modeling is a set of practices that support effective communication and understanding within Agile Process and Project Management disciplines. It prioritizes simplicity, flexibility, and active stakeholder participation to create models that are just good enough for the current stage of the project.

Agile Planning

Agile planning refers to the iterative and flexible approach used in Agile process and project management disciplines. It is a dynamic process that focuses on collaboration, adaptability, and continuous improvement to deliver value to the customer.

In Agile planning, the project requirements and scope are not fixed at the beginning of the project. Instead, they are continuously refined and adjusted based on customer feedback, changing market needs, and evolving business priorities. This iterative approach allows teams to respond quickly to changes and deliver a high-quality product that meets the customer's needs.

Agile planning involves breaking down the project into smaller, manageable iterations called sprints. Each sprint typically lasts for a few weeks and involves planning, executing, and reviewing the work. During the sprint planning phase, the team collaborates to define the goals and objectives for the upcoming sprint, prioritize the work, and estimate the effort required for each task.

Throughout the project, the team engages in frequent communication and collaboration to address any issues or obstacles that arise. They use various Agile planning techniques, such as user stories, burndown charts, and daily stand-up meetings, to monitor progress, identify risks, and make necessary adjustments to the plan.

By embracing Agile planning, teams can achieve greater transparency, flexibility, and customer satisfaction. The iterative nature of Agile planning allows for continuous feedback and improvement, enabling the team to deliver value early and often.

Agile Principles

Agile principles are foundational concepts that guide the Agile process and project management disciplines. These principles serve as a set of values and beliefs that shape the mindset and behavior of Agile practitioners.

Agile principles are guided by the Agile Manifesto, which emphasizes individuals and interactions, working solutions, customer collaboration, and responding to change. These principles are applicable to various Agile methodologies, such as Scrum, Kanban, and Lean, enabling teams to deliver high-quality products and services efficiently.

The first Agile principle focuses on satisfying the customer through early and continuous delivery of valuable software. This principle encourages frequent releases, ensuring that customers receive working solutions that meet their evolving needs.

The second principle emphasizes welcoming changes in requirements, even during later stages of development. Agile teams view changes as opportunities to add value and deliver better outcomes, facilitating customer collaboration and competitive advantage.

The third principle highlights the importance of delivering working solutions collaboratively. Agile project management promotes self-organizing teams that have the authority and capability to make decisions and adapt to evolving requirements.

The fourth principle emphasizes continuous attention to technical excellence and good design. Agile teams prioritize effective engineering practices, such as automated testing and refactoring, to ensure the long-term maintainability and scalability of their products.

The final principle encourages teams to regularly reflect on their effectiveness and make necessary improvements. Through continuous feedback and retrospectives, Agile teams focus on optimizing their processes, enhancing productivity, and fostering a culture of learning and innovation.

Agile Project Management

Agile Project Management is a disciplined approach to managing projects that aims to deliver high-quality products or services in a flexible and interactive manner. It embraces the principles of the Agile Manifesto, which values individuals and interactions, working products, customer collaboration, and responding to change.

Unlike traditional project management methodologies, Agile Project Management focuses on iterative and incremental development, allowing for frequent delivery of tangible results. The process is characterized by short development cycles, called sprints or iterations, which typically last for one to four weeks. Each iteration includes all the necessary activities for developing and delivering a specific set of features or functionality.

The Agile Project Management framework is often implemented using various methodologies, such as Scrum, Kanban, or Lean. These methodologies provide specific guidelines and practices for managing project teams, prioritizing work, planning and executing iterations, and reviewing and adapting the project's direction.

Key features of Agile Project Management include constant communication and collaboration with stakeholders, embracing change as a natural part of the project, and delivering incremental value to the customer throughout the project's lifecycle. The project team, consisting of cross-functional members, works closely together and self-organizes to ensure the successful delivery of the product or service.

Agile Release Planning

Agile release planning is a fundamental activity within the Agile process and project management disciplines. It involves identifying and prioritizing the features, user stories, and tasks that will be included in each release of an Agile project. Release planning helps the team establish a roadmap for delivering value to stakeholders in an iterative and incremental manner.

The primary goal of Agile release planning is to achieve a balance between delivering valuable functionality and managing project constraints such as time, budget, and resources. It requires collaboration and effective communication between the product owner, the development team, and other stakeholders to ensure that the project's objectives are met.

Agile Release Train

The Agile Release Train (ART) is a key element of the Scaled Agile Framework (SAFe) and is used in Agile Process and Project Management disciplines. An ART is a long-lived, self-organizing, and cross-functional team of Agile teams that helps to deliver value to the customer on a regular cadence.

An ART is composed of multiple Agile teams, typically 5-12 teams, that work together to deliver a large and complex solution. These teams are organized around a common mission or business objective and are responsible for the end-to-end delivery of value. They are cross-functional, meaning they have all the necessary skills and capabilities to design, develop, test, and deliver the solution.

The ART operates on a fixed timebox known as a Program Increment (PI) which is typically 8-12 weeks long. During a PI, the teams work together in a synchronized manner to deliver a set of features and capabilities. The PI planning event is a key ceremony where all teams come together to plan and align their work for the upcoming PI.

The ART is led by a Release Train Engineer (RTE) who acts as a servant leader and facilitator for the teams. The RTE ensures that the teams are aligned, focused, and have everything they need to deliver value. They also help to remove any impediments that may arise during the PI.

Agile Retrospective

An Agile Retrospective is a structured and focused meeting that takes place at the end of each iteration or sprint in an Agile project. It is a key component of the Agile process and project management disciplines.

The main purpose of an Agile Retrospective is to enable the team to reflect on their recent work and identify opportunities for improvement. It provides a platform for the team to discuss what went well, what didn't go well, and what could be done differently in future iterations. The retrospective meeting helps to foster a culture of continuous improvement within the team, allowing them to learn from their experiences and make adjustments as needed.

During an Agile Retrospective, the team members share their observations, insights, and suggestions in an open and collaborative manner. The focus is on identifying actionable items that can be implemented in the next iteration to enhance the team's performance. The retrospective should be a safe space, where everyone feels comfortable and encouraged to speak their mind, without fear of judgment or blame.

The Agile Retrospective typically follows a structured format, such as the "Start, Stop, Continue" model or the "Glad, Sad, Mad" technique. These frameworks provide a framework for the discussion and help to ensure that all relevant topics are covered. The facilitator, often the Scrum Master or Agile Coach, guides the team through the retrospective, ensuring that everyone has a voice and that the meeting stays on track.

Agile Risk Management

Agile Risk Management is a key component of the Agile Process and Project Management disciplines. It involves identifying, assessing, and managing risks throughout the project lifecycle in an agile environment.

Risk management in the Agile framework focuses on early and continuous identification of risks to prevent them from becoming major issues later on. It promotes a proactive approach to risk management rather than a reactive one, allowing teams to address potential problems as soon as they arise.

One of the key principles of Agile Risk Management is collaboration. It encourages open communication and involvement of all team members in risk identification and resolution. By involving everyone in the process, the team can leverage their collective knowledge and experience to identify risks more effectively and come up with appropriate mitigation strategies.

Another important aspect of Agile Risk Management is prioritization. In an agile project, risks are assessed based on their impact and probability, and prioritized accordingly. This allows the team to focus their efforts on addressing the most critical risks first, ensuring that the project remains on track and delivers the expected outcomes.

Agile Risk Management also emphasizes adaptability and flexibility. As new risks emerge or existing risks evolve, the team should be ready to adjust their risk mitigation strategies and plans accordingly. This continuous monitoring and adaptation ensure that potential risks are constantly evaluated and managed in a dynamic and changing project environment.

Agile Scaling

Agile Scaling refers to the capability of expanding and adapting Agile methodologies and practices to larger and more complex projects, organizations, or teams. It is a strategic approach that allows for the effective collaboration, coordination, and delivery of multiple Agile teams working on a shared set of goals and objectives.

In the context of Agile Process and Project Management disciplines, Agile Scaling focuses on addressing the challenges faced when implementing Agile in larger and more diverse environments. It aims to enable organizations to achieve agility at scale by providing a framework that ensures alignment and synchronization among multiple Agile teams, while still maintaining flexibility and responsiveness.

Agile Scrum

Agile Scrum is a project management framework that follows the Agile process. It emphasizes flexibility, collaboration, and iterative development to deliver high-quality products in a short period of time. Scrum, as a subset of Agile, provides a lightweight approach to managing and controlling complex projects.

Agile Scrum is centered around small, self-organizing, cross-functional teams called Scrum teams. These teams work in short time periods, called sprints, typically lasting 1-4 weeks. During each sprint, the team focuses on delivering a specific set of features or functionalities based on the priorities set by the product owner.

One of the key principles of Agile Scrum is incremental delivery. Instead of delivering a complete product at the end of a long development cycle, Agile Scrum promotes the delivery of working increments of a product at the end of each sprint. This allows stakeholders to provide feedback early on and for the product to evolve and adapt based on changing requirements and market conditions.

The Agile Scrum process is highly collaborative. Daily stand-up meetings, known as daily scrums, are held to provide transparency, enhance communication, and address any roadblocks or impediments. The product owner works closely with the development team to define and prioritize the product backlog, which is a list of features or user stories. The product backlog is continuously refined and reprioritized throughout the project.

In summary, Agile Scrum is a project management framework that emphasizes flexibility, collaboration, and incremental delivery. It enables teams to adapt to changing requirements and deliver value to customers in a timely manner.

Agile Team

An Agile team is a cross-functional group of individuals who work together collaboratively to deliver high-quality products or services using Agile methodologies. In the context of Agile process and project management disciplines, an Agile team is essential for successful project execution and delivery.

An Agile team typically consists of different roles including but not limited to a product owner, scrum master, developers, testers, and other stakeholders. These team members collaborate closely to understand the project requirements, plan iterations or sprints, and iteratively develop and deliver value to customers.

The Agile team follows the principles and practices of Agile methodologies such as Scrum, Kanban, or Lean. They embrace iterative and incremental development approaches, allowing them to quickly respond to changing requirements, incorporate feedback, and continuously improve their work.

The Agile team operates in a self-organizing manner, meaning that they collectively decide how to plan, track, and execute their work. They collaborate daily through ceremonies like daily stand-ups, sprint planning, sprint reviews, and retrospectives. This close collaboration enables them to increase transparency, improve communication, and foster a sense of ownership and accountability.

The Agile team promotes a culture of trust, openness, and continuous learning. They value face-to-face communication, frequent feedback, and adapting to change. They prioritize delivering value to customers and meeting their needs by frequently releasing deliverables that can be tested, reviewed, and improved upon.

In conclusion, an Agile team is a essential component in Agile project management, playing a crucial role in delivering high-quality products or services that meet customer expectations.

Agile Testing

Agile testing is a fundamental aspect of the Agile project management discipline, which focuses on iterative development and frequent feedback to deliver high-quality software products.

Agile testing involves a collaborative approach where testers, developers, and business stakeholders work closely together throughout the software development lifecycle. It emphasizes continuous and early testing to ensure the product meets customer requirements and expectations. The goal of Agile testing is to identify defects and issues as early as possible, enabling quick feedback and corrective actions.

Agile Transformation

Agile Transformation refers to the process of adopting and implementing Agile principles and practices within an organization or project management discipline. It is a systematic approach that involves a shift in mindset, processes, and organizational culture to enable faster and more efficient delivery of high-quality products or services.

Agile Transformation recognizes the limitations of traditional project management methodologies and emphasizes flexibility, collaboration, and continuous improvement. It is based on the belief that requirements and solutions evolve through the collaborative effort of self-organizing and cross-functional teams. Agile Transformation promotes close customer collaboration, iterative development, and fast feedback cycles.

Agile Values

Agile values are a set of principles that guide the Agile Process and Project Management disciplines. These values promote collaboration, flexibility, adaptability, and customer-centricity, ultimately resulting in better project outcomes.

The first Agile value is "Individuals and interactions over processes and tools." This means that the focus should be on effective communication, collaboration, and teamwork rather than relying solely on predefined processes and tools. By valuing individuals and their interactions, Agile teams can better understand and meet the needs of their customers and stakeholders.

The second Agile value is "Working software over comprehensive documentation." Instead of spending excessive time and effort on extensive documentation, Agile teams prioritize delivering working software that meets the immediate needs of the customers. This value emphasizes the importance of continuous delivery and feedback, allowing for faster iterations and improvements based on real-world usage.

The third Agile value is "Customer collaboration over contract negotiation." Agile teams aim to establish close partnerships with their customers, involving them throughout the project lifecycle to ensure that the delivered software fully addresses their requirements and expectations. This value encourages regular customer feedback, fostering a more dynamic and responsive development process.

The fourth Agile value is "Responding to change over following a plan." Agile emphasizes the need for flexibility and adaptability in response to changing business and market dynamics. Rather than rigidly following a plan, Agile teams embrace change and continuously adjust their approach to maximize value delivery. This value helps mitigate risks and ensures that project outcomes remain aligned with evolving customer and market needs.

Agile Workshop

An Agile Workshop is a collaborative session that involves a group of individuals, typically consisting of project stakeholders, development team members, and business representatives, who come together to explore, learn, and apply Agile principles and practices in the context of project management.

The workshop is designed to foster communication, knowledge sharing, and active engagement among participants, with the goal of improving the overall effectiveness and efficiency of the Agile process. It serves as a platform for teams to enhance their understanding of Agile concepts and techniques, and to discuss and resolve any challenges or issues they may encounter during the project lifecycle.

Agile

Agile is a project management approach that emphasizes flexibility, adaptability, and collaboration to deliver a high-quality product efficiently. It is based on iterative and incremental development, allowing project teams to respond quickly to changes in requirements and customer feedback.

Agile focuses on delivering value to the customer through regular and frequent product increments, promoting continuous improvement and transparency. It empowers cross-functional, self-organizing teams to make decisions collectively, fostering creativity and innovation.

Alignment

Alignment in the context of Agile Process and Project Management disciplines refers to the synchronization of project goals, objectives, and actions with the overall strategic direction and objectives of the organization. It involves ensuring that the project and its deliverables are aligned with the broader vision, values, and priorities of the organization.

In an Agile environment, alignment is facilitated through ongoing collaboration and communication between the project team, stakeholders, and senior leaders. This is achieved through various Agile ceremonies such as sprint planning, daily stand-ups, sprint reviews, and retrospectives, where team members discuss and align their work with the organization's strategic goals and priorities.

Backlog Grooming

Backlog grooming, also known as backlog refinement or backlog management, is a crucial activity in the Agile process and project management disciplines. It involves regularly reviewing and organizing the items in the backlog to ensure their relevance, clarity, and readiness for implementation.

The backlog, in Agile methodology, refers to a prioritized list of features, user stories, or tasks that need to be completed during the project. Backlog grooming helps the project team to maintain a well-maintained and evolving backlog that aligns with the project goals and objectives.

During backlog grooming, the product owner, scrum master, and development team collaborate to review and refine the backlog items. This process involves adding, modifying, or removing items based on changing requirements, stakeholder feedback, or project priorities.

The main objectives of backlog grooming are:

- Ensuring the backlog items are clear, concise, and well-defined, enabling the development team to understand them easily.

- Estimating the effort required to implement each item, allowing for better planning and prioritization.

- Prioritizing the backlog items based on their value, dependencies, and urgency, enabling the team to work on the most valuable and critical items first.

- Breaking down larger items into smaller, manageable pieces that can be completed within a single iteration or sprint.

- Updating the backlog based on new information, requirements, or insights gained during the project.

By regularly grooming the backlog, the project team can maintain a clear understanding of the work that needs to be done and ensure that the backlog remains up-to-date and relevant. This practice improves the overall efficiency, predictability, and success of Agile projects.

Backlog Item

A backlog item in the context of Agile Process and Project Management disciplines refers to a specific task, feature, or requirement that has been identified and prioritized for inclusion in the product backlog. The product backlog is a dynamic list of all the work that needs to be done on a project, containing items that are yet to be completed, as well as those that have already been completed.

Backlog items are usually described in the form of user stories, which are short, simple, and focused statements that capture a specific functionality or feature from the end-user's perspective. These user stories serve as placeholders for conversations that will happen in the future between the development team and the stakeholders, helping to keep the user's needs and expectations at the forefront of the development process.

Backlog Items

The term "backlog items" refers to a list or collection of tasks, features, or requirements that are prioritized and still need to be completed within an Agile process, primarily in the context of project management disciplines. These items are usually recorded in an Agile project management tool, such as a digital board or a physical Kanban board, and serve as a central repository for work planning and tracking.

Backlog items can include various types of work, such as user stories, bug fixes, technical debt, or even strategic initiatives. They help Agile teams to collaborate, prioritize, and deliver value incrementally by breaking down complex projects into smaller, manageable units of work. The items are typically described with a concise title, a brief description, and relevant acceptance criteria that provide clarity on the desired outcome.

Backlog Refinement

Backlog Refinement is a crucial practice in the Agile Process and Project Management disciplines. It involves continuously updating, prioritizing, and clarifying items in the product backlog to ensure the development team has a clear understanding of what needs to be done.

During backlog refinement, the product owner and the development team collaboratively review and analyze the user stories or items in the backlog. They assess the size, complexity, and dependencies of each item and make adjustments to the priority and order in which they will be worked on. This process helps establish a shared understanding of the work to be done and ensures the backlog remains relevant and manageable.

The main objective of backlog refinement is to break down user stories and backlog items into smaller, more detailed tasks. By doing so, the team can better estimate the effort required to complete each task and plan accordingly. This decomposition also facilitates successful sprint planning, as the development team can more accurately determine the amount of work they can commit to within a single sprint.

Additionally, backlog refinement helps identify any missing or unclear requirements, allowing the product owner to provide the necessary clarifications. This collaborative effort between the product owner and the development team ensures everyone is on the same page and reduces the chances of misunderstandings and rework down the line.

In conclusion, backlog refinement is an ongoing activity that aims to keep the product backlog up-to-date, well-defined, and manageable. It plays a vital role in Agile Process and Project Management by ensuring the development team has a clear understanding of the work ahead and enabling effective sprint planning and execution.

Backlog

A backlog, in the context of Agile Process and Project Management disciplines, refers to a prioritized list of requirements, features, or tasks that need to be completed within a project. It serves as a dynamic repository of work that is constantly maintained and updated throughout the project lifecycle.

The backlog typically consists of user stories, which are concise, independent, and testable descriptions of desired functionality from the perspective of end-users or stakeholders. These user stories act as placeholders for conversations between the development team and the stakeholders, helping to establish a shared understanding of the project goals and objectives.

The backlog is prioritized based on the value it brings to the project and the needs of the stakeholders. The items at the top of the backlog represent the highest priority and provide the most immediate value to the project. As the project progresses, the backlog is continuously refined and reprioritized based on changing requirements, emerging insights, and stakeholder feedback. This allows the project team to adapt and respond to evolving needs and ensure that the most valuable work is always being addressed.

During Agile ceremonies such as sprint planning or backlog grooming sessions, the project team collaboratively reviews the backlog and selects the items that will be included in the upcoming sprint. The team estimates the effort required to complete each item, which helps in determining the sprint capacity and establishing a realistic sprint goal.

Behavior-Driven Development (BDD)

Behavior-Driven Development (BDD) is a software development approach that emphasizes collaboration between different stakeholders to define and prioritize the behavior of a software system. It is aligned with the principles of Agile processes and is commonly used in project management disciplines.

In BDD, the behavior of the software system is described in terms of scenarios that specify the desired outcome or behavior. These scenarios are written in a structured, non-technical language, such as Gherkin syntax, which is easily understandable by both technical and non-technical stakeholders.

BDD follows a collaborative approach where stakeholders, including business analysts, developers, testers, and product owners, work together to define and refine these scenarios. This collaborative process helps in ensuring that all stakeholders have a shared understanding of the software system's behavior, reducing misunderstandings and improving the overall quality of the software.

In BDD, scenarios are often written using a Given-When-Then format. The Given step sets up the initial state of the scenario, the When step represents the action or event that triggers the behavior, and the Then step defines the expected outcome or behavior. These scenarios serve as executable specifications and can be automated to validate the behavior of the software.

By using BDD, Agile teams can enhance communication, collaboration, and alignment between different stakeholders. It promotes a shared understanding of the software's behavior, enables early discovery of requirements and potential issues, and facilitates iterative development and delivery. BDD also helps in reducing rework and increasing overall software quality by ensuring that the software meets the expected behavior and addresses the needs of the stakeholders.

Behavioral Metrics

Behavioral metrics in the context of Agile Process and Project Management disciplines refer to the measurements and analysis of individuals' and teams' behavior and performance to enhance project delivery and team collaboration. These metrics provide valuable insights into the behavioral dynamics within the Agile team, helping to identify areas of improvement and guide decision-making processes to optimize team productivity.

Agile methodologies emphasize the importance of self-organizing teams and continuous improvement. Behavioral metrics play a crucial role in monitoring and tracking team dynamics, communication patterns, and individual performance to foster a healthy and collaborative work environment. These metrics can include measurements of task completion time, participation in Agile ceremonies, adherence to Agile practices, team engagement level, and overall team morale.

Big Visible Charts

Big Visible Charts, also known as BVC, are a visual representation of data and information used in Agile Process and Project Management disciplines. These charts are large and prominently displayed in the team's workspace, providing real-time updates on the progress and status of the project.

One common type of BVC used in Agile is the Kanban board. This chart is divided into columns that represent different stages of the project, such as "To Do," "In Progress," and "Done." Each task or user story is represented by a sticky note or card, which is moved across the columns as progress is made. This visual representation allows team members to quickly assess the status of the project and identify any bottlenecks or issues.

Bottleneck

A bottleneck in the context of Agile Process and Project Management disciplines refers to a point in a workflow where the flow of work is impaired or restricted, leading to a slower overall pace of progress. It is a constraint or limitation that hinders the efficiency of the process and prevents work from being completed at an optimal rate.

Identifying bottlenecks is crucial in Agile Project Management as it helps to uncover areas that require attention or improvement. By recognizing and addressing these bottlenecks, project teams can enhance their productivity and delivery outcomes.

Burn-Down Chart

A burn-down chart is a visual representation that tracks the progress of work completed and work remaining in an agile project. It is a popular tool used in agile process and project management disciplines to monitor and communicate the project's progress.

The burn-down chart typically plots two axes: time and work. The vertical axis represents the amount of work remaining, while the horizontal axis indicates the time elapsed or the project's duration. The chart starts with the initial amount of work estimated for the project and shows the progress made over time.

The burn-down chart provides a clear and concise overview of the project's status, enabling stakeholders to understand the project's progress at a glance. It helps the team identify trends, track velocity, and make data-driven decisions to optimize their workflow and meet project objectives.

By tracking the actual progress against the planned progress, the burn-down chart helps the team identify any discrepancies or delays, allowing for timely adjustments and course corrections. It also helps in visualizing the remaining work, allowing team members to prioritize tasks and ensure the project stays on track.

The burn-down chart is a collaborative tool that encourages transparency and accountability within the team. It facilitates communication and enables stakeholders to actively participate in the project by providing a shared understanding of the project's progress and challenges.

In summary, a burn-down chart is an essential tool in agile process and project management. Its visual representation of work completed and work remaining helps the team and stakeholders monitor, analyze, and optimize the project's progress and outcomes.

Burn-Up Chart

A burn-up chart is a visual tool commonly used in Agile Process and Project Management disciplines to track and communicate the progress of a project. It provides a graphical representation of the work completed against the work planned over time, allowing teams to assess their progress and make data-driven decisions to ensure project success.

The burn-up chart typically consists of two axes: the x-axis represents time, divided into iterations or sprints, while the y-axis represents the amount of work completed. The desired scope of the project is represented by the upper line, which shows the total work planned. As the project progresses, the lower line displays the actual work completed, reflecting the cumulative value of the completed tasks or user stories.

A burn-up chart gives project teams and stakeholders a transparent view of how the project is rapidly progressing towards the goal or target line. By comparing the planned work with the completed work, it becomes easier to identify any deviations early on and take corrective actions without delays. This chart also helps in managing scope changes effectively by clearly showing the impact on the project timeline and work completed.

In addition, the burn-up chart is a valuable communication tool. It allows project managers to provide updates on project progress to stakeholders, facilitating meaningful discussions about potential risks and changes in project direction. It provides a shared understanding of the project status and promotes collaboration across team members, enabling them to make data-driven decisions to optimize their work and achieve project goals.

Burndown Chart

A burndown chart is a visual representation of the amount of work left to be completed in an Agile project. It is used in Agile process and project management disciplines to track the progress of tasks and to forecast the project's completion date.

The burndown chart usually has two axes - the horizontal axis represents time, typically in iterations or sprints, and the vertical axis represents the remaining work. The remaining work is usually measured in story points, a unit of estimation used in Agile projects.

The chart is created by plotting the remaining work against the time axis. At the beginning of the project, the chart starts with the total estimated work for the project. As the project progresses, the team updates the chart by subtracting the completed work from the total estimated work, resulting in the remaining work. The chart visually shows the trend of work completion and helps the team to identify whether they are on track or falling behind.

By tracking the burndown chart, the team can determine the project's velocity, which is the rate at which they are completing work. This information allows for more accurate forecasting and helps the team to make informed decisions about scope, deadlines, and resource allocation. It also provides transparency and visibility to stakeholders, enabling them to understand the project's progress and potentially adjust their expectations or priorities.

Cadence

In the context of Agile Process and Project Management disciplines, cadence refers to the rhythm or pattern followed in the execution of tasks and activities within a project. It provides a structured and predictable flow of work, allowing team members to synchronize their efforts and maintain a sense of momentum.

Cadence encompasses various elements of the Agile methodology, such as sprint cycles, iterative development, and regular meetings. It helps teams establish a consistent pace and rhythm, ensuring that work is completed within the defined time frames and with optimal efficiency.

Capability Maturity Model (CMM)

The Capability Maturity Model (CMM) is a widely used framework for assessing and improving the maturity level of process and project management practices in organizations, particularly those following the Agile methodology. It provides a structured approach to measuring and evaluating an organization's ability to reliably and consistently achieve project goals and deliver high-quality products and services.

The CMM consists of five maturity levels, each representing a higher level of process capability and organizational maturity. These levels are as follows:

Level 1 - Initial: Processes are unpredictable and ad hoc, with little documentation or process discipline. Success is dependent on individual heroics and good luck.

Level 2 - Managed: Basic project management processes are established and used to effectively plan, track, and control project activities. Project success is now repeatable and more predictable.

Level 3 - Defined: Standardized processes are developed and documented, enabling consistency and scalability across projects. There is a focus on process improvement and organizational learning.

Level 4 - Quantitatively Managed: Processes are now quantitatively controlled and measured, using metrics to monitor and improve performance. Predictability and efficiency are further enhanced.

Level 5 - Optimizing: Continuous process improvement is integrated into the organization's culture, creating a learning organization that continually adapts and evolves its practices to achieve higher levels of performance and customer satisfaction.

By following the CMM, organizations can gain a comprehensive understanding of their current process maturity level, identify areas for improvement, and implement targeted initiatives to advance to higher levels of maturity. This ultimately leads to improved project success rates, increased customer satisfaction, and better overall organizational performance.

Capability

A capability, in the context of Agile Process and Project Management disciplines, can be defined as the combination of knowledge, skills, and resources that an individual or a team possesses to successfully accomplish a specific task or achieve a desired outcome within the Agile framework.

Agile processes require individuals and teams to possess certain capabilities to effectively execute and deliver projects. These capabilities include technical expertise, domain knowledge, communication skills, collaboration abilities, problem-solving skills, adaptability, and a deep understanding of Agile principles and methodologies.

Having the right capabilities is crucial for Agile project success as they enable individuals and teams to respond quickly and effectively to changes, incorporate feedback, and deliver high-quality results within short iterations or sprints. Moreover, capabilities help in identifying and managing risks, making informed decisions, and continuously improving the project delivery process.

Agile teams typically comprise members with diverse capabilities that complement each other. This diversity brings a wider range of perspectives, enhances creativity, and fosters innovation within the team. Furthermore, Agile organizations emphasize developing and enhancing the capabilities of their team members through continuous learning, training, and knowledge sharing.

Hence, in Agile Process and Project Management disciplines, capabilities are vital assets that enable individuals and teams to effectively navigate the complexities of Agile projects, deliver value to stakeholders, and achieve project objectives.

Capacity Planning

Capacity planning in the context of Agile Process and Project Management disciplines refers to the process of determining the optimal allocation of resources, including time, people, and equipment, to meet the demands of an Agile project efficiently and effectively. It involves assessing the team's capacity and workload, considering factors such as team member availability, skill sets, and task requirements, to ensure a balanced and sustainable workload for the team.

This planning process takes into account the organization's goals, project objectives, and available resources, along with the team's capabilities and limitations. The goal of capacity planning is to prevent overloading or underutilization of resources, which can lead to inefficiencies, delays, and poor project outcomes.

22

In an Agile context, capacity planning is particularly important due to the iterative nature of Agile projects, where priorities and requirements can change dynamically. It involves continuously evaluating and adjusting resource allocation based on changing project needs and team capabilities. By properly managing capacity, Agile teams are better equipped to deliver quality work within the project's scope, timeline, and budget.

Effective capacity planning relies on accurate and up-to-date data, ongoing communication and collaboration within the team, and the use of Agile project management tools and techniques. It requires regular monitoring and analysis of team performance, identifying bottlenecks, and adjusting resource allocation as needed to optimize productivity and ensure the successful delivery of Agile projects.

Capacity

Capacity refers to the maximum amount of work that a team or individual can handle within a given time frame. In the context of Agile Process and Project Management disciplines, capacity planning is crucial for determining how much work can be accomplished during each iteration or sprint.

During capacity planning, the team takes into consideration various factors such as the team's size, skill sets, availability, and the amount of work already committed to. By accurately estimating their capacity, the team can set realistic goals for each iteration, ensuring that they don't overcommit or underdeliver.

Ceremonies

A ceremony in the context of Agile Process and Project Management disciplines refers to a scheduled event or meeting that follows a specific format and aims to promote collaboration, communication, and alignment within a project. These ceremonies are designed to facilitate the Agile principles and values, promoting transparency, delivering value to the customer, and allowing for continuous improvement.

There are several key ceremonies commonly used in Agile methodologies, including the Daily Stand-up or Daily Scrum, Sprint Planning, Sprint Review, and Sprint Retrospective. The purpose of each ceremony varies:

The Daily Stand-up, also known as the Daily Scrum, is a short, time-boxed meeting where team members share updates on their progress, discuss any impediments or challenges they are facing, and identify potential solutions. This ceremony helps to promote collaboration and ensures that all team members are aware of ongoing work and potential blockers.

Sprint Planning is a ceremony where the team defines the scope of work for a sprint, sets clear goals and objectives, and identifies the tasks required to achieve those goals. It involves the Product Owner and the Development Team, ensuring alignment between business requirements and technical implementation.

The Sprint Review is a demonstration of the work completed during a sprint to the stakeholders and customers. It provides an opportunity for feedback and validation, allowing for continuous improvement and adjustments to meet changing requirements.

The Sprint Retrospective is a reflective session where the team reflects on the previous sprint, identifies what went well and areas for improvement, and defines actionable items to enhance their processes and practices. This ceremony fosters a culture of continuous learning and growth.

Through these ceremonies, Agile processes and project management disciplines promote collaboration, maximize transparency, and drive efficiency and value delivery.

Ceremony

A ceremony, in the context of Agile process and project management disciplines, refers to a specific event or meeting that is conducted with a defined purpose and structure. These ceremonies play a crucial role in facilitating effective communication, collaboration, and synchronization among team members, stakeholders, and the project itself.

Agile methodologies, such as Scrum, incorporate several ceremonies throughout the project lifecycle to ensure transparency, adaptability, and continuous improvement. The most common ceremonies in Agile project management include:

The Daily Stand-up: Also known as a Daily Scrum, this short daily meeting brings the entire team together to discuss progress, challenges, and plans for the day. Each team member answers three questions: "What did I accomplish yesterday?", "What will I work on today?", and "Are there any obstacles in my way?" This ceremony promotes transparency, accountability, and cross-team collaboration.

The Sprint Planning: This ceremony precedes the start of each sprint and is attended by the entire project team, including the Product Owner. The team collaboratively decides which product backlog items (PBIs) will be worked on during the upcoming sprint and establishes a sprint goal. Sprint Planning enables the team to set realistic expectations and plan their work effectively.

The Sprint Review: At the end of every sprint, the project team conducts the Sprint Review. This ceremony includes a demonstration of the completed features, allowing stakeholders to provide feedback and make necessary adjustments to the product backlog. The Sprint Review helps validate the team's work and ensures that the product is meeting stakeholders' expectations.

The Retrospective: Following the Sprint Review, the Retrospective is conducted to reflect on the recently completed sprint and identify areas for improvement. The team discusses what went well, what didn't, and how they can make adjustments in the next sprint. The Retrospective encourages continuous learning and iterative improvement throughout the project.

Cognitive Biases

Cognitive biases refer to systematic patterns of deviation from rationality when individuals make judgments and decisions. In the context of Agile Process and Project Management disciplines, cognitive biases can have a significant impact on the effectiveness and efficiency of the decision-making process.

Agile processes rely heavily on collaborative decision-making and quick adaptation to change. However, cognitive biases can hinder this process by distorting perceptions, influencing judgments, and leading to irrational decision-making. Some common cognitive biases that can affect Agile processes and project management include confirmation bias, anchoring bias, availability bias, and optimism bias.

Confirmation bias occurs when individuals favor information that confirms their existing beliefs or hypotheses, leading to a tendency to overlook or dismiss contradictory evidence. This bias can hinder the ability to objectively evaluate alternative solutions or adapt to changing requirements in Agile projects.

Anchoring bias refers to the tendency to rely too heavily on the first piece of information encountered (the "anchor") when making judgments or decisions. This bias can limit creativity and exploration of new ideas, as team members may become fixated on initial estimates or assumptions.

Availability bias occurs when individuals rely on readily available information or examples that come to mind easily, rather than considering a broader range of possibilities. This bias can lead to overemphasizing certain risks or solutions based on recent experiences or prominent examples, potentially overlooking valuable insights or opportunities.

Optimism bias refers to the tendency for individuals to be overly optimistic about the outcomes of their actions or projects. This bias can lead to underestimating the effort, time, or resources required for project tasks, resulting in delays or inadequate planning.

Collaboration

Collaboration in the context of Agile Process and Project Management disciplines refers to the practice of individuals and teams working together to achieve a common goal. It emphasizes the importance of open communication, sharing of knowledge and resources, and collective decision-making.

Within Agile, collaboration is a core principle that enables teams to respond to change, deliver value to customers, and continuously improve. It is based on the idea that the whole team is responsible for the success of the project, and that each individual brings unique skills and perspectives to the table.

Collaborative Culture

A collaborative culture in the context of Agile Process and Project Management disciplines refers to a work environment that encourages open communication, cooperation, and shared responsibility among team members. It emphasizes the value of working together to achieve common goals and encourages cross-functional collaboration throughout the project lifecycle.

In a collaborative culture, individuals from different disciplines and roles, such as developers, designers, testers, and stakeholders, come together to collaborate and share their expertise in order to deliver high-quality products or services. This culture fosters a sense of trust and respect among team members, enabling them to effectively communicate, solve problems, and make decisions collectively.

Collaboration in Agile Process and Project Management disciplines is typically facilitated through various practices and tools, such as daily stand-up meetings, sprint planning sessions, and collaborative software platforms. These practices encourage team members to openly share their progress, challenges, and ideas, allowing for continuous improvement and adaptation throughout the project.

A collaborative culture also values feedback and encourages individuals to provide constructive criticism and suggestions for improvement. This feedback-driven approach fosters a culture of learning and growth, where mistakes are seen as opportunities for improvement rather than failures.

In summary, a collaborative culture in Agile Process and Project Management disciplines promotes effective teamwork, open communication, and shared responsibility among team members. It creates an environment where individuals can collaborate, learn from each other, and collectively deliver successful projects.

Collaborative Ideation Platforms

Collaborative Ideation Platforms are digital tools and platforms designed to facilitate the generation and exchange of ideas in the context of Design Thinking disciplines. These platforms enable individuals or teams, irrespective of geographical limitations, to contribute ideas, insights, and feedback, thereby fostering a collaborative environment for ideation and problem-solving.

The key objective of Collaborative Ideation Platforms is to promote inclusiveness and maximize the diversity of perspectives during the ideation process. The platforms typically provide a structured framework or framework templates, such as design challenges or problem statements, to guide participants through the ideation process.

Through these platforms, participants can employ various ideation techniques, such as brainstorming, mind mapping, or card sorting, to generate and capture ideas. The platforms often facilitate real-time collaboration, allowing multiple individuals to contribute ideas simultaneously and allowing participants to comment, build upon, or offer feedback on each other's ideas.

Collaborative Ideation Platforms also provide functionalities for organizing and filtering ideas to enable efficient evaluation and analysis. Participants can vote or rate ideas based on their viability, feasibility, or desirability, helping to identify and prioritize the most promising concepts for further development and implementation.

In summary, Collaborative Ideation Platforms leverage digital technologies to enable remote and collaborative ideation within the framework of Design Thinking disciplines. By providing a structured and inclusive environment for idea generation, these platforms facilitate the exploration of diverse perspectives and ultimately support the development of innovative solutions to complex challenges.

Collaborative Ideation Workspaces

A collaborative ideation workspace is a physical or virtual environment that is specifically designed to facilitate the creative and collaborative process of generating and developing ideas. It is an essential component of the Design Thinking disciplines, which are used to solve complex problems and drive innovation.

Within a collaborative ideation workspace, individuals or teams can come together to brainstorm ideas, share knowledge and insights, and explore potential solutions. The environment is intentionally designed to promote open communication, trust, and a sense of psychological safety, which are crucial for fostering creativity and encouraging participants to think outside the box.

Physical collaborative ideation workspaces often feature flexible furniture arrangements, such as movable tables and chairs, whiteboards or chalkboards for visualizing ideas, and plenty of wall space for displaying and organizing information. These spaces may also include various tools and materials, such as sticky notes, markers, and prototyping materials, to support the ideation process.

Virtual collaborative ideation workspaces, on the other hand, are digital platforms or applications that allow individuals or teams to collaborate remotely. These platforms typically provide features such as virtual whiteboards, chat functionalities, and document sharing capabilities. Remote participants can contribute ideas, provide feedback, and collaborate in real time, regardless of their physical location.

Collaborative Ideation

Collaborative Ideation is a key component of the Design Thinking process. It refers to the collaborative generation and exploration of ideas within a group or team. The goal of Collaborative Ideation is to foster creativity and innovation by leveraging the collective knowledge, perspectives, and experiences of all participants.

During Collaborative Ideation, individuals come together to brainstorm, share ideas, and build upon each other's thoughts. This process encourages active collaboration and cross-pollination of ideas, leading to the development of diverse and novel solutions to complex problems. It involves creating a safe and inclusive space where everyone's ideas are valued, and no judgment or criticism is allowed.

The Collaborative Ideation process typically involves various techniques and activities, such as brainstorming sessions, mind mapping, rapid prototyping, and design studios. These methods help stimulate creativity, break down silos, and promote a culture of open-mindedness and curiosity.

Collaborative Ideation is effective because it harnesses the power of collective intelligence. By bringing together individuals with different backgrounds, expertise, and perspectives, it maximizes the chances of generating breakthrough ideas and insights. It also encourages participants to build on each other's ideas, leading to the emergence of more refined and robust solutions.

In summary, Collaborative Ideation is a fundamental aspect of Design Thinking that emphasizes active collaboration, inclusiveness, and the exploration of diverse ideas. By leveraging the collective intelligence of a group, it helps unlock creative solutions and drive innovation.

Collaborative Problem Solving

Collaborative Problem Solving in the context of Design Thinking disciplines can be defined as a process that involves multiple individuals working together to identify, understand, and address complex problems or challenges. It is a collaborative approach that encourages diverse perspectives, encourages free-flowing communication, and embraces iterative problem-solving.

Collaborative Problem Solving in Design Thinking begins with a shared understanding of the problem at hand. This involves gathering insights from various stakeholders and users through methods such as interviews, observations, or surveys. Through empathizing with the target audience and identifying their needs, the team gains a deeper understanding of the problem they are trying to solve.

Once the problem is defined, the collaborative team engages in ideation, generating a wide range of creative solutions without judgment. This divergent thinking allows for a rich exploration of possibilities and enables the team to think outside the box. Through these brainstorming sessions, the team combines their unique expertise and experiences to uncover innovative ideas.

After the ideation phase, the team moves into the convergence phase. Here, they narrow down the generated ideas and select the most promising ones based on feasibility, desirability, and viability. Through open and constructive conversations, the team debates and discusses the merits of each idea before making a collective decision.

The final step in Collaborative Problem Solving is prototyping and testing. The team creates quick prototypes to visualize and test their solutions, gathering feedback from users, stakeholders, or experts. This iterative process allows for continuous refinement and improvement based on real-world insights, ultimately leading to a more effective and user-centric solution.

Collaborative Problem-Solving Apps

A collaborative problem-solving app is a digital tool that facilitates teamwork and collaboration among individuals or groups in the context of the Design Thinking disciplines. These apps are specifically designed to support the process of problem-solving by implementing the principles of collaborative thinking and leveraging the power of technology to enhance teamwork and creativity.

These apps provide a platform for users to work together, brainstorm ideas, analyze problems, and propose solutions in a collaborative and systematic manner. They often incorporate various features such as real-time collaboration, digital whiteboards, virtual sticky notes, and interactive visualization tools to facilitate the exchange of ideas and foster effective communication among team members.

By using collaborative problem-solving apps, teams can overcome geographical barriers and work together efficiently regardless of their physical location. These apps enable remote teams to collaborate effectively and ensure that all team members have equal opportunities to contribute and participate in the problem-solving process.

The key benefits of using collaborative problem-solving apps include improved team communication, enhanced creativity, increased productivity, and the ability to capture and record ideas and insights in a digital format. These apps also promote inclusivity and diversity by allowing individuals from different backgrounds and perspectives to contribute and collaborate on problem-solving tasks.

In summary, collaborative problem-solving apps are powerful digital tools that empower individuals and teams to work together in a structured and collaborative manner. They promote effective communication, foster creativity, and facilitate the generation of innovative solutions in the context of the Design Thinking disciplines.

Collaborative User Research

Collaborative user research is a critical component of the Design Thinking process, which involves multidisciplinary teams working together to gain a comprehensive understanding of users and their needs. It is a methodical approach that brings together different perspectives and expertise to generate insights that inform the design and development of innovative solutions.

During collaborative user research, cross-functional teams collaborate in conducting research activities such as interviews, observations, and surveys to gather rich qualitative and quantitative data about users. This collaborative approach ensures that different team members can contribute different insights and interpretations of the collected data, resulting in a holistic understanding of users and their context.

The collaborative nature of this research method also promotes empathy and fosters an inclusive and participatory environment. It encourages team members to actively listen to each other's perspectives, challenge assumptions, and collectively make sense of the research findings. This collaborative process helps to uncover deep insights, uncover latent needs, and ideate potential solutions that address the identified user problems.

The insights gained from collaborative user research serve as a foundation for the iterative design process, enabling teams to create user-centered solutions that resonate with real user needs and expectations. By involving diverse team members in the research process, organizations can leverage a variety of skills, experiences, and perspectives to ultimately create more innovative and impactful products and services.

Collaborative Whiteboarding Tools

Collaborative whiteboarding tools are digital platforms that enable teams to visually ideate, brainstorm, and collaborate in real-time during the design thinking process. These tools facilitate the sharing and creation of ideas, concepts, and solutions through an interactive virtual whiteboard.

Designed specifically for the design thinking disciplines, collaborative whiteboarding tools aim to enhance the collaboration and creativity of multidisciplinary teams. These tools allow team members to contribute their thoughts, concepts, and drawings on a shared canvas, promoting collective understanding and co-creation. The virtual whiteboard often replicates the experience of a physical whiteboard, providing a familiar interface for participants.

With collaborative whiteboarding tools, teams can overcome the limitations of physical whiteboards by working together remotely and asynchronously. These tools offer features such as sticky notes, drawing tools, shapes, text boxes, and color options to facilitate the expression of ideas. Additionally, participants can leverage features like commenting, voting, and annotation to provide feedback and refine concepts.

The real-time collaboration aspect of these tools allows team members to see each other's contributions instantly, fostering a sense of engagement, motivation, and accountability. This instant feedback loop accelerates the design thinking process, enabling teams to iterate and refine their ideas more efficiently.

In conclusion, collaborative whiteboarding tools are essential for design thinking disciplines as they empower teams to collaboratively ideate, visualize, and refine their concepts. By leveraging these tools, teams can enhance their creativity, communication, and overall problem-solving capabilities, regardless of physical location or time constraints.

Collective Ownership

Collective Ownership in the context of Agile Process and Project Management disciplines refers to the principle that emphasizes shared responsibility and accountability for the project or product among the entire team. It promotes a collaborative approach to decision-making and encourages all team members to feel a sense of ownership and investment in the successful outcome of the project.

Under the concept of Collective Ownership, each team member contributes to the overall success of the project by taking ownership of their individual tasks and collaborating with others to achieve the team's goals. Instead of assigning specific tasks to specific individuals, Collective Ownership allows for flexibility and adaptability within the team, enabling members to contribute to multiple areas and take on tasks based on their skills, availability, and interest.

Commitment

The concept of commitment plays a crucial role in the Agile Process and Project Management disciplines. In these disciplines, commitment refers to the dedication and responsibility of individuals and teams to complete tasks and achieve project goals.

In Agile Process, commitment is demonstrated through the commitment to deliver value to the customer continuously. This means that the team members are dedicated to delivering working software in short iterations or sprints. They commit to completing the tasks they have selected for the sprint and delivering the agreed-upon features or functionalities at the end of the sprint.

In Agile Project Management, commitment is also important. The project manager and team members commit to delivering the project scope within the agreed-upon budget and timeline. This commitment involves establishing realistic and achievable goals, breaking down the project into manageable tasks, and allocating resources effectively.

Commitment in Agile Process and Project Management is not just about completing tasks or delivering a product. It also involves actively participating in team collaboration, continuously improving processes, and adapting to changing requirements. Individuals and teams demonstrate commitment by taking ownership of their work, openly communicating progress and challenges, and actively seeking solutions to overcome obstacles.

In summary, commitment in Agile Process and Project Management disciplines refers to the dedication and responsibility of individuals and teams to deliver value to the customer, complete tasks within the agreed-upon scope, and actively participate in collaboration and improvement efforts.

Complexity

Complexity may be defined as the measure of the intricacy or difficulty of a task, process, or system within the context of Agile Process and Project Management disciplines. It refers to the level of intricacy and interdependencies within a project's various elements, including tasks, requirements, stakeholders, and resources.

Within Agile Process and Project Management, complexity can arise from various factors, such as the size and scope of the project, the number of stakeholders involved, the level of uncertainty or ambiguity in requirements, and the degree of technological or organizational intricacy. As complexity increases, the challenges associated with project planning, execution, and delivery also tend to escalate.

Concept Mapping Software

Concept mapping software is a digital tool used within the context of Design Thinking disciplines to visually depict, organize, and connect complex ideas and concepts. It provides a platform for individuals or teams to structure their thoughts, brainstorm ideas, and create a visual representation of the relationships between different concepts.

By allowing users to create diagrams, maps, or flowcharts, concept mapping software aids in the exploration, analysis, and synthesis of concepts, facilitating the process of problem-solving and design ideation. It serves as a means to visually represent the connections and hierarchies between ideas in a non-linear format, promoting a holistic view of the problem or design challenge at hand.

Constructive Critique

Design Thinking is a problem-solving approach that is centered around understanding and empathizing with users, generating creative ideas, and iterating through a cycle of prototyping and testing to develop innovative solutions. It is a discipline that combines analytical and creative thinking to tackle complex problems and uncover new opportunities. Design Thinking is characterized by a human-centered focus, which means that the needs, desires, and behaviors of the end-users are at the forefront of the design process. Through thorough research and observation, designers aim to deeply understand the users' perspectives and experiences to gain valuable insights. This empathetic understanding enables designers to identify pain points, challenges, and unmet needs, which then serve as foundations for problem statements and design opportunities. The next phase of Design Thinking involves ideation, where designers generate a multitude of ideas to address the identified problem or challenge. This step encourages divergent thinking, as designers explore a wide range of possible solutions without judgment or limitation. By embracing ambiguity and pushing boundaries, designers aim to come up with innovative and creative concepts that can potentially disrupt existing paradigms. Following the ideation phase, designers move on to prototyping and testing. Here, they create tangible representations of their ideas, such as physical models, wireframes, or interactive prototypes. These prototypes are then evaluated and tested with potential users to gather feedback and insights. Through this iterative process, designers refine and improve their solutions based on the feedback received, continuously striving for user-centric designs. Design Thinking's interdisciplinary approach encourages collaboration among individuals with diverse backgrounds, expertise, and perspectives. It fosters a culture of continuous learning, adaptation, and user-centered innovation. Design Thinking can be applied to a wide range of contexts and challenges, including product design, service design, experience design, organizational design, and social innovation. In conclusion, Design Thinking is a problem-solving approach that prioritizes user empathy, creative ideation, prototyping, and testing. It combines analytical thinking with a deep understanding of human needs and desires to develop innovative solutions. It is a discipline that encourages collaboration, iteration, and continuous improvement to create impactful and meaningful designs.

Contextual Adaptation

Contextual Adaptation refers to the process of designing and adapting a solution to meet the specific needs and constraints of a particular context or user group. It is an essential element of the Design Thinking methodology, which focuses on understanding and empathizing with users, and developing innovative solutions that address their unique challenges and requirements.

The process of Contextual Adaptation involves gathering deep insights about the users and their context through research and observation. This includes understanding their behaviors, preferences, and the environmental factors that influence their interactions and experiences. By immersing themselves in the users' world, designers gain a comprehensive understanding of the challenges they face and the opportunities for improvement.

Once the user insights are gathered, designers use this knowledge to generate and refine ideas for potential solutions. These ideas are then adapted and tailored to the specific context, taking into account the cultural, societal, and technological factors that may impact the effectiveness and usability of the solution.

Throughout the design process, designers continuously test and iterate their solutions in collaboration with the users, using feedback to refine and adapt the design to better match the users' needs and expectations. This iterative approach ensures that the final solution is a result of a deep understanding of the users and their context, and is optimized to provide maximum value and impact.

Contextual Analysis

Contextual analysis is a method used within the discipline of Design Thinking to gather insights and understand the context in which a problem or challenge exists. It involves examining the broader environment, including the social, cultural, economic, and technological factors that may impact the problem at hand.

By conducting a contextual analysis, designers can gain a deeper understanding of the users they are designing for and the constraints they may face in their particular context. This understanding helps designers generate more meaningful and relevant solutions that address the real needs and behaviors of the users. Through observation, interviews, and research, designers can uncover important insights about the users' preferences, motivations, values, and goals.

Contextual Awareness

Contextual Awareness refers to the deep understanding of the overall context in which a design problem exists, including the environment, circumstances, users, and their needs. In Design Thinking disciplines, this concept is crucial for creating effective and meaningful solutions.

Designers practicing Contextual Awareness employ various research methods such as direct observation, interviews, and immersion in order to gain insights and empathy towards the end users. They seek to identify the specific needs, motivations, and behaviors of the users, as well as the broader social, cultural, and environmental factors that may influence the problem or solution.

Continuous Delivery

Continuous Delivery is a software development approach that focuses on delivering working software to end users in a frequent and efficient manner. It is closely aligned with Agile processes and project management disciplines, allowing for rapid and iterative development cycles.

In the context of Agile, Continuous Delivery emphasizes the importance of delivering value to customers at every stage of the development process. This is achieved through the use of automated testing, continuous integration, and continuous deployment practices. By breaking down software development into smaller, manageable increments, teams are able to respond more quickly to changes and feedback, resulting in higher-quality software and greater customer satisfaction.

Continuous Deployment

Continuous Deployment is a software development practice that focuses on delivering code changes to production environments frequently and automatically. It is a key aspect of the Agile process and project management disciplines.

In Continuous Deployment, the entire software release process is automated, including testing, integration, and deployment. This allows for small, incremental changes to be deployed quickly and continuously, rather than in larger, infrequent releases. This approach helps ensure that the latest working version of the software is always available to end users.

Continuous Exploration

Continuous Exploration is a core practice in Agile Process and Project Management disciplines that involves the ongoing and iterative exploration of ideas and proposed solutions to uncover valuable insights, gather feedback, and ensure alignment with business goals. This practice emphasizes the importance of continuously engaging with stakeholders, conducting market research, and actively seeking opportunities for improvement throughout the project lifecycle.

By continuously exploring and validating assumptions, Agile teams can quickly adapt to changing customer needs, market trends, or technical constraints to make informed decisions and deliver value early and often. This approach encourages collaboration and transparency, allowing teams to gather diverse perspectives, challenge assumptions, and validate ideas through user feedback, analytics, and market research.

Continuous Improvement

Continuous Improvement is a fundamental principle of Agile Process and Project Management disciplines. It refers to the ongoing effort to enhance processes, products, and services by systematically identifying and addressing areas for improvement.

Continuous Improvement is based on the belief that there is always room for improvement, no matter how well a process or project is currently performing. It involves a cyclical approach, where feedback and learnings from previous iterations are used to inform future iterations. This iterative process enables teams to incrementally enhance their performance and deliver greater value to stakeholders.

Continuous Improvement is deeply ingrained in the Agile mindset and is supported by various practices and tools. It encourages individuals and teams to regularly reflect on their work, gather feedback, and identify areas for improvement. This can include reviewing and adapting processes, identifying bottlenecks or inefficiencies, and seeking ways to streamline workflows.

Continuous Improvement is not limited to addressing only the problems or shortcomings of a process or project. It also encompasses identifying and capitalizing on opportunities for innovation and growth. By fostering a culture of continuous improvement, Agile teams are empowered to experiment, take risks, and explore new ideas to deliver better outcomes.

Continuous Integration

Continuous Integration (CI) is a fundamental practice in Agile Process and Project Management disciplines. It involves the frequent merging of code changes from multiple developers into a shared repository. The primary aim of CI is to address the potential integration problems that arise when developers work in isolation for an extended period.

CI entails automating the build and testing processes, ensuring that code changes are regularly integrated into a shared codebase, and regression tests are executed to validate the integration. Developers commit their code changes to a version control system, triggering the CI server to build the application, run unit tests, and conduct static code analysis.

CI serves as an early warning system by instantly detecting integration issues caused by conflicting changes, build failures, or broken functionalities. It provides rapid feedback, allowing developers to address these issues promptly. Furthermore, CI enhances collaboration and promotes a cohesive team environment. It encourages developers to communicate frequently, merge their changes frequently, and resolve integration conflicts promptly.

By integrating code continuously, CI reduces the time and effort required for code integration and stabilization at the end of a project. It enables developers to identify and fix issues earlier in the development process, avoiding costly rework or delays. Additionally, CI supports the practice of continuous delivery by ensuring that the software is always in a releasable state.

In conclusion, Continuous Integration is a crucial practice in Agile Process and Project Management. It facilitates early problem detection, improves collaboration, and enhances overall development efficiency, ultimately leading to higher quality software products.

Continuous Testing

Continuous Testing refers to the practice of regularly and iteratively testing software throughout the Agile development process in order to detect defects and ensure its quality. It is an integral part of Agile Project Management and helps to deliver high-quality software products in an Agile environment.

In the Agile methodology, software is developed in short iterations known as sprints. Continuous Testing involves testing the software at every stage of the development process, including during the sprint planning, coding, and deployment phases. It is a proactive approach that emphasizes the early detection and prevention of defects, rather than waiting until the end of the development cycle for testing.

Conway's Law

Conway's Law, within the context of Agile Process and Project Management disciplines, refers to the observation made by computer scientist Melvin Conway that states, "organizations which design systems...are constrained to produce designs which are copies of the communication structures of these organizations."

In other words, Conway's Law suggests that the structure of an organization directly influences the structure of the systems or software that it develops. This law highlights the intricate relationship between communication patterns and the resulting product. Specifically, it implies that the communication paths within an organization will manifest themselves in the product's architecture and design.

Cross-Functional Team

A cross-functional team, in the context of Agile Process and Project Management disciplines, refers to a group of individuals who possess different skills, expertise, and knowledge from various functional areas within an organization. These functional areas can include departments such as development, design, testing, marketing, and support.

Unlike traditional teams, which are often comprised of individuals from the same functional area, cross-functional teams are formed with the purpose of promoting collaboration, communication, and diversity of perspectives to enhance the overall effectiveness of project delivery.

Cross-Functional

Cross-Functional refers to a collaborative approach within the Agile Process and Project Management disciplines. It involves bringing together individuals with diverse skill sets and expertise from different departments or functional areas to work towards a common goal or objective.

In an Agile environment, teams are typically self-organizing and empowered to make decisions. Cross-functional teams are formed by pulling together individuals with complementary skills, such as software developers, quality assurance testers, designers, business analysts, and project managers, among others. Each team member brings their unique perspective and capabilities, contributing to the success of the project.

Cumulative Flow Diagram

A Cumulative Flow Diagram (CFD) is a visual representation of the flow of work in an Agile process or project management discipline. It provides a historical record of work progress and can be used to track and analyze the efficiency and effectiveness of the flow.

The CFD consists of a graph with two axes: time on the horizontal axis and the number of work items on the vertical axis. Each area on the graph represents a stage or phase of the workflow, with the width of the area representing the time spent in that stage and the height representing the number of work items currently in that stage.

The CFD is updated continuously throughout the project or process, reflecting changes in the number of work items in each stage over time. It allows team members, stakeholders, and managers to get a clear understanding of the work in progress, identify bottlenecks or areas of improvement, and make data-driven decisions to optimize the flow of work.

The CFD can also indicate the cycle time, which is the time taken for an item to move from one stage to another. By analyzing the CFD, teams can identify variations in cycle time and take actions to reduce it, ultimately improving the overall efficiency and delivery of the project or process.

Customer Collaboration

Customer collaboration is a key principle in Agile Process and Project Management disciplines. It refers to the active involvement and collaboration between the development team and the customer throughout the project lifecycle.

In the Agile approach, the customer plays a vital role in shaping the project's direction and outcome. The customer provides valuable input, requirements, feedback, and priorities to ensure a successful product delivery. This collaborative approach ensures that the project meets the customer's needs and expectations, resulting in a higher level of customer satisfaction.

Customer Value

Customer value refers to the perceived benefit or worth that a customer receives from a product or service. Within the context of Agile Process and Project Management disciplines, customer value is a key concept that guides decision-making and prioritization of work.

Agile methodologies, such as Scrum, prioritize delivering customer value at frequent intervals during a project. This approach emphasizes collaboration, adaptability, and iterative development, enabling teams to respond to changing customer needs and preferences. By delivering small increments of functionality with each iteration, Agile teams can gather feedback from customers and stakeholders, ensuring that the product or service aligns with their expectations.

The Agile process focuses on understanding the customer's requirements and utilizing feedback loops to continuously refine and improve the product. Customer value is determined by identifying and addressing the needs, desires, and pain points of the target market. The Agile team works closely with customers to gather and prioritize user stories, allowing them to deliver features that provide maximum value to the end-users.

In Agile Project Management, customer value plays a crucial role in prioritizing the product backlog. The product owner, in collaboration with stakeholders, evaluates and ranks the user stories based on their potential to deliver customer value. This ensures that the team focuses on delivering the most valuable features early in the project, maximizing the return on investment (ROI) for the customer.

Cycle Time

Cycle Time is a metric used in Agile Process and Project Management disciplines to measure the time taken to complete a specific task or activity in a project. It represents the total time it takes for an item to move through a specific process or workflow, from start to finish. This metric provides valuable insights into the efficiency and productivity of the project team and helps in identifying bottlenecks and areas for improvement.

For Agile projects, Cycle Time is particularly important as it helps in managing and tracking the progress of work items, such as user stories or tasks, in the iterative development process. By measuring the time it takes to complete each work item, the team can assess its ability to deliver value quickly and make data-driven decisions to optimize their workflow and resources.

Daily Meeting

A daily meeting, also known as a daily stand-up or daily scrum, is a short and focused gathering of team members involved in an Agile process or project management disciplines. The purpose of this meeting is to provide a regular opportunity for team members to discuss their progress, identify any obstacles or challenges they are facing, and coordinate their efforts towards achieving the project goals.

The daily meeting typically takes place at the same time every day and follows a structured format. Each team member shares three key pieces of information: what they accomplished since the last meeting, what they plan to accomplish by the next meeting, and any impediments that are hindering their progress. The meeting serves as a synchronization point for the team, ensuring everyone is aligned and aware of each other's work.

Daily Scrum

The Daily Scrum is a key component of the Agile Process and Project Management disciplines. It is a brief and focused team meeting that takes place every day during a sprint, typically lasting no longer than 15 minutes. The purpose of the Daily Scrum is to provide an opportunity for the team members to synchronize their work, discuss progress, and identify any potential obstacles or issues that may hinder the achievement of the sprint goal.

During the Daily Scrum, each team member answers three fundamental questions:

- What did I do yesterday to help the team achieve the sprint goal?

- What am I planning to do today to contribute to the team's progress?

- Are there any obstacles or challenges that are impeding my progress?

By answering these questions, the team members gain a shared understanding of the progress made, the challenges faced, and the planned actions for the day. This allows for increased transparency and collaboration within the team, ensuring that everyone is aligned and focused on achieving the sprint goal.

It is important to note that the Daily Scrum is not a status update or a problem-solving meeting. It is a time-boxed event where the team members quickly share information and identify any potential obstacles. Any in-depth discussions or problem-solving should be taken offline to prevent derailing the meeting and wasting everyone's time.

Daily Standup

The Daily Standup is a key component of the Agile Process and Project Management disciplines. It is a short, focused meeting where the project team gathers to discuss progress, challenges, and plans for the day. The purpose of the Daily Standup is to promote transparency, collaboration, and efficiency within the team.

During the Daily Standup, each team member provides a brief update on three key items: what they accomplished since the last meeting, what they plan to achieve today, and any obstacles or dependencies they are facing. The meeting typically lasts around 15 minutes, and it is essential that every team member actively participates and stays engaged.

The Daily Standup serves several important functions. Firstly, it allows team members to share their progress and align their activities with the overall project goals. By regularly communicating their accomplishments and plans, team members can identify any potential overlaps or conflicts in their work and make necessary adjustments. Secondly, the meeting provides an opportunity to address and resolve any issues or obstacles faced by team members. By openly discussing challenges, the team can collectively brainstorm solutions and ensure no one is stuck or delayed in their work. Lastly, the Daily Standup fosters collaboration and a sense of shared responsibility among team members. It encourages open communication and accountability, as each team member is aware of what their colleagues are working on and can offer support or guidance when needed.

Data Visualization

Data visualization is the graphical representation of data using visual elements such as charts, graphs, and maps. It is an essential component of Design Thinking disciplines as it helps to analyze, understand, and communicate complex information in a clear and concise manner.

In the Design Thinking process, data visualization plays a crucial role in the early stages of problem-solving. It enables designers and teams to gather, organize, and make sense of data, transforming it into meaningful insights. By visually representing data, patterns, trends, and relationships can be identified more easily, allowing for informed decision-making and innovation.

Decentralization

Decentralization, in the context of Agile Process and Project Management disciplines, refers to the distribution of decision-making authority and accountability across individuals or teams within an organization. It is a fundamental principle of Agile methodologies that promotes flexibility, collaboration, and adaptability.

In a decentralized Agile environment, power is shared, and decisions are made by the people closest to the work, rather than being dictated by a central authority. This enables teams to respond quickly to changing requirements and empowers individuals to take ownership of their work and make informed decisions.

Decoupling

Decoupling in the context of Agile Process and Project Management disciplines refers to the practice of creating a separation between different components, modules, or elements of a software system or project. This separation allows for greater flexibility, scalability, and maintainability, ultimately helping teams to deliver projects more efficiently.

In the Agile approach, decoupling is often used as a means to achieve modular and loosely-coupled architecture. By breaking down a project into smaller independent components, teams can focus on developing and testing each component separately, reducing dependencies and allowing for parallel work. This modular approach enables teams to work on different parts of a project concurrently, increasing productivity and speeding up the development process.

Definition Of Done

In the context of Agile Process and Project Management disciplines, the Definition of Done refers to a concise set of criteria that must be met in order for a user story or task to be considered complete. It acts as a shared agreement among the team members regarding the quality and completeness of the work delivered during a sprint.

The Definition of Done typically includes both technical and non-technical requirements. Technical requirements ensure that the work meets the necessary coding, testing, and documentation standards, while non-technical requirements cover aspects such as usability, user acceptance, and adherence to any relevant regulatory or compliance standards.

Definition Of Ready

The Definition of Ready is a concept utilized in Agile Process and Project Management disciplines. It refers to a set of criteria or conditions that a user story must meet before it can be considered ready for implementation in an Agile project. This concept helps in ensuring that the user stories are well-defined, understood, and feasible, thus enabling the team to work efficiently and effectively in delivering the expected value.

A user story is considered ready when it satisfies certain criteria that make it actionable and ready for implementation. These criteria can vary based on the project and team preferences, but commonly include aspects such as:

- Clear and Specific: The user story should be concise, unambiguous, and specific in its description. It should convey a clear understanding of the desired functionality or feature.

- Independent: The user story should be independent of other stories and should not have any dependencies that can hinder its implementation or cause delays.

- Estimable: The user story should be understandable enough for the team to estimate its complexity and effort accurately. This helps in planning and prioritizing tasks effectively.

- Testable: The user story should be written in a way that its acceptance criteria can be defined and used as a basis for testing. This ensures that the outcome of the story can be validated against the defined criteria.

- Ready for Development: The user story should have all the required information, including any necessary designs, wireframes, or acceptance criteria, to start the development process without any ambiguity or uncertainty.

By establishing a Definition of Ready, teams can ensure that the user stories are actionable and well-prepared, minimizing rework, misunderstandings, and delays during the development phase. It serves as a guideline for the team to prioritize, plan, and execute the project efficiently within the Agile framework.

Deliverable

The term "deliverable" refers to a tangible or intangible item that is produced as a result of completing a specific task or milestone within the Agile Process and Project Management disciplines. It can take various forms, such as documents, software components, prototypes, or other materials that are created to meet the requirements of a project.

In Agile Process, deliverables are typically produced iteratively and incrementally throughout the project duration. This approach allows for continuous feedback and collaboration between the project team and stakeholders, ensuring that the final deliverable meets the desired objectives and requirements. Each deliverable represents a checkpoint or milestone in the project's progress, enabling the team to track and measure their accomplishments.

When it comes to Project Management, deliverables play a crucial role in defining the scope of work, setting expectations, and managing stakeholders' needs. They provide a means to communicate progress, showcase completed tasks, and highlight any dependencies or issues that may arise. Additionally, deliverables serve as a reference point for quality assurance and testing activities, ensuring that the project's outputs meet the specified standards and fulfill the intended purpose.

In conclusion, the term "deliverable" represents a tangible or intangible item produced within the Agile Process and Project Management disciplines. These items serve as milestones, checkpoints, and communication tools throughout the project, helping to ensure that the desired objectives and requirements are met.

Dependency

A dependency is a relationship between two or more tasks or activities in a project where the completion or progress of one task is dependent on the completion or progress of another task. In the context of Agile Process and Project Management disciplines, dependencies play a crucial role in managing project timelines and ensuring the smooth execution of project tasks.

In Agile methodologies, such as Scrum, dependencies are identified and managed through various techniques. One common technique is the use of a dependency backlog, where all the dependencies are listed and prioritized. This allows the project team to have a clear understanding of the dependencies and their impact on the project timeline.

Design Sprint

A Design Sprint is a highly structured and time-constrained process that follows the principles of Design Thinking, aimed at solving complex problems and rapidly prototyping innovative solutions. It involves a diverse group of stakeholders working collaboratively over a set period of time, typically five days, to explore, ideate, and validate ideas.

The Design Sprint begins with a "problem framing" phase, where the team identifies and clarifies the challenge they are trying to address. This phase includes activities such as creating a shared understanding of the problem, conducting research, and defining clear goals and success metrics.

Next, the team engages in a series of ideation and sketching exercises to generate a wide range of possible solutions. These exercises often involve activities like brainstorming, mind mapping, and sketching interfaces or storyboards.

After ideation, the team goes through a process of converging and selecting the most promising ideas. This phase includes techniques like dot voting, where each team member selects their favorite ideas, and a "heat map" exercise to visually represent the consensus of the group.

Once a set of ideas have been selected, the team creates low-fidelity prototypes, often using tools like pen and paper or digital prototyping software. These prototypes aim to quickly test and validate assumptions about the proposed solutions.

Finally, the team conducts user testing, where real users interact with the prototypes and provide feedback. This feedback is used to refine and iterate on the designs, allowing the team to make informed decisions about which solutions to pursue further.

Design Thinking

Design Thinking is a problem-solving approach that emphasizes empathy, collaboration, and experimentation to create innovative solutions. It is widely used in the Agile Process and Project Management disciplines to tackle complex challenges and drive successful outcomes.

In the context of Agile, Design Thinking helps teams adopt a user-centric mindset by understanding the needs and preferences of the end-users. It encourages cross-functional collaboration and iterative feedback loops to continuously improve the product or service being developed.

Design Thinking encompasses five stages: empathize, define, ideate, prototype, and test. During the empathize phase, teams aim to understand the users' pain points and motivations. In the define phase, they synthesize the gathered insights to define the problem or challenge at hand. Ideation involves generating a wide range of creative solutions, while prototyping allows the teams to visualize and test their ideas in a low-fidelity manner.

The final stage, test, involves gathering feedback from users and stakeholders to refine the solutions iteratively. This iterative approach allows teams to validate assumptions, uncover new opportunities, and make informed decisions based on real user insights.

By employing Design Thinking within the Agile Process and Project Management disciplines, organizations can foster a culture of innovation and collaboration. It helps teams focus on creating value for the end-users and encourages adaptability in an ever-changing market landscape.

DevOps

DevOps is a practice in Agile Process and Project Management disciplines that emphasizes collaboration, integration, automation, and communication between software developers and IT operations teams. It aims to break down the traditional barriers between development and operations by promoting a culture of shared responsibility and continuous improvement.

In the Agile context, DevOps focuses on delivering software faster and more reliably through the automation of build, test, deployment, and monitoring processes. By bringing together development and operations teams early in the software development lifecycle, DevOps enables faster feedback cycles, better collaboration, and the ability to respond quickly to customer feedback.

Development Team

The development team is a group of individuals responsible for executing and delivering the tasks and objectives of a project in the context of Agile Process and Project Management disciplines. This team is composed of cross-functional members with the required skills and expertise, ensuring the ability to fulfill the project requirements effectively and efficiently.

Within an Agile framework, the development team collaborates closely with the product owner and scrum master to understand and prioritize the features and user stories. They actively engage in the agile ceremonies, such as sprint planning, daily stand-ups, sprint reviews, and sprint retrospectives, to ensure transparency and continuous improvement.

Disciplined Agile Delivery (DAD)

Disciplined Agile Delivery (DAD) is an agile framework that combines multiple agile and lean methods into one comprehensive approach for delivering high-quality software solutions. It is specifically designed to address the complexities and challenges faced by large-scale enterprises and projects, while still remaining true to the principles of agile development.

DAD recognizes that every project is unique and requires flexibility in its approach. It provides a customizable toolkit of processes, practices, and guidelines, allowing teams to tailor their approach based on the specific needs and constraints of their project. This flexibility is achieved by drawing upon a wide range of agile and lean methods, including Scrum, Kanban, Lean, SAFe, and Agile Modeling.

One of the key features of DAD is its focus on the entire delivery lifecycle, from project initiation to deployment and beyond. It provides guidance and support for all phases of delivery, including requirements exploration, architecture, coding, testing, deployment, and release management. This holistic approach ensures that teams consider all aspects of the delivery process, including governance, risk management, and enterprise-level concerns.

Another important aspect of DAD is its emphasis on tailoring agile practices to fit the needs of the project. It recognizes that not all agile practices are applicable or suitable for every project, and encourages teams to select and adapt practices based on their specific context. This enables teams to strike a balance between agility and control, ensuring that they are able to deliver high-value solutions while still meeting the needs of their stakeholders.

Emergent Design

Emergent design, in the context of Agile Process and Project Management disciplines, refers to a principle that emphasizes the continuous evolution and refinement of the design of a software system throughout its development lifecycle. It recognizes that designing a complex system upfront can be challenging and that a better understanding of the requirements and constraints emerges as the project progresses.

Unlike traditional sequential approaches, where the design is fixed at the beginning and any changes or adjustments are costly and time-consuming, emergent design embraces flexibility and adaptability. The focus is on delivering working software incrementally, enabling the team to gather feedback and learn from it to inform their design decisions.

The Agile Manifesto values "Responding to change over following a plan," and emergent design aligns with this mindset. Instead of investing significant effort in detailed upfront design, Agile teams prioritize working closely with stakeholders, constantly collaborating, and incorporating feedback to validate and refine their design choices.

The process of emergent design involves starting with a simple and flexible design that supports the initial requirements, building the system incrementally, and continuously making informed decisions based on evolving knowledge. It emphasizes the importance of refactoring, a practice of improving the design of existing code without changing its external behavior, to maintain the system's integrity and adaptability as new requirements emerge.

By embracing emergent design, Agile teams can effectively manage project complexity and uncertainty. They leverage short feedback loops, frequent interactions, and incremental delivery to ensure the system's design aligns with the evolving needs of stakeholders, allowing for a more responsive and successful software development process.

Emergent

Emergent refers to a concept in Agile Process and Project Management disciplines which emphasizes adaptability and flexibility in response to evolving requirements and circumstances.

In Agile Process Management, emergence refers to the phenomena where new insights, ideas, and solutions naturally arise during the iterative and incremental development process. This is in contrast to traditional Waterfall methodologies, where all requirements and project specifications are defined upfront and changes are difficult to incorporate once the project is underway. Through the emergent nature of Agile, teams can continuously refine and improve their understanding of the project as they progress, leading to a more effective and successful outcome.

Empirical Process Control

Empirical Process Control is a fundamental concept in Agile Process and Project Management disciplines. It refers to a systematic and iterative approach that emphasizes frequent inspection and adaptation of processes and projects based on empirical evidence.

In Agile, the key principle behind empirical process control is the assumption that complex activities, such as software development projects, are highly unpredictable and subject to change. Therefore, it is crucial to continuously assess and adjust the processes and projects based on real-time feedback and observations, rather than relying on detailed plans developed upfront.

Empiricism

Empiricism is a fundamental principle in Agile Process and Project Management disciplines, focusing on the importance of empirical evidence and feedback for decision-making and progress evaluation.

In the context of Agile, empiricism refers to the three pillars that support the framework of Scrum – transparency, inspection, and adaptation. Transparency promotes openness and visibility of information related to the project, allowing all stakeholders to have a common understanding of the progress and challenges. Inspection emphasizes continuous monitoring and assessment of the work and processes, enabling early detection of risks or impediments. Adaptation encourages flexibility and responsiveness in adjusting the project plan and approach based on the insights gained from the inspection.

These pillars are rooted in the belief that knowledge and solutions emerge from experience and experimentation rather than solely relying on predictive plans and assumptions. Empiricism promotes a mindset of continuous learning and improvement, recognizing that uncertainty and complexity are inherent in projects, and adaptation based on empirical evidence leads to better outcomes.

In Agile Process and Project Management, empirical approaches such as incremental and iterative development, frequent feedback loops, and empirical process control are relied upon to manage uncertainties and guide decision-making. This approach allows teams to adapt and respond to changing requirements, prioritize value delivery, and optimize processes through frequent inspection and adaptation cycles.

Empowerment

First

tag: Empowerment in the context of Agile Process and Project Management disciplines refers to the delegation of authority, responsibility, and decision-making power to individuals or teams within an organization. It is a fundamental principle that promotes self-organization, collaboration, and continuous improvement. Through empowerment, individuals or teams are given the autonomy and trust to make decisions and take ownership of their work. They are empowered to plan, prioritize, and execute tasks in a way that best aligns with the project goals and objectives. This allows for greater flexibility and adaptability in responding to changes and uncertainties that may arise during the project lifecycle. Empowerment also encourages individuals or teams to take initiative, innovate, and explore new ideas. It fosters a culture of accountability, where individuals or teams are responsible for their actions and outcomes. In this way, empowerment promotes learning, growth, and personal development. Second

tag: In Agile Project Management, empowerment is a key factor in achieving high-performing teams and successful project outcomes. It enables teams to be self-organizing, where members collectively determine how to best achieve their goals and deliver value to stakeholders. Empowerment allows for quick decision-making, as authority is decentralized and distributed among team members. Furthermore, empowerment supports the Agile principle of customer collaboration, as it enables teams to engage directly with stakeholders and make decisions based on their feedback and requirements. This leads to greater customer satisfaction and a more iterative and incremental delivery process. Overall, empowerment plays a crucial role in Agile Process and Project Management by promoting autonomy, accountability, collaboration, and continuous improvement. It empowers individuals or teams to take ownership, make decisions, and drive the success of Agile projects.

Epic

Agile Process is a project management methodology that focuses on iterative and incremental development, allowing for adaptability and flexibility. It emphasizes collaboration, communication, and transparency among team members. The Agile Process is centered around the idea of delivering value to customers through rapid and continuous feedback and improvement.

Project Management disciplines within the Agile Process framework involve a set of practices and principles that guide the planning, execution, monitoring, and control of projects. These disciplines prioritize customer satisfaction, emphasize self-organizing and cross-functional teams, and promote adaptive planning and evolutionary development. Project Management in Agile aims to empower teams to deliver high-quality software products or services in a timely and efficient manner.

Epics

An Epic is a large body of work that can be broken down into a set of smaller, more manageable User Stories. It is a high-level requirement or goal that represents a significant deliverable for a project. Epics are often used in Agile processes, such as Scrum, to help manage and prioritize work.

In the context of Agile Project Management, Epics are used to capture and communicate the overall vision and objectives of a project. They provide a way to organize and group related User Stories, allowing teams to focus on delivering value incrementally. Epics also help to facilitate planning and estimation by providing a framework for breaking down complex work into more manageable pieces.

Estimation

Estimation, in the context of Agile Process and Project Management disciplines, refers to the process of predicting or estimating the time, effort, resources, and costs required to complete a specific task, feature, or project. It involves evaluating and quantifying the work that needs to be done and providing an approximate schedule or timeline for its completion.

Estimation plays a crucial role in Agile methodologies as it helps in prioritizing and planning the work. It enables the project team to effectively allocate resources, track progress, and make informed decisions. By providing estimates, the team gains insight into the complexity and scope of the work, allowing them to set achievable goals and manage expectations.

Experiential Learning

Experiential learning is a pedagogical approach that emphasizes hands-on and practical experiences as a means of acquiring knowledge and understanding in the context of design thinking disciplines.

In the context of design thinking disciplines, experiential learning involves actively engaging students in real-world experiences and challenges. It encourages them to explore, experiment, and learn through direct involvement and observation. This approach recognizes that design thinking is not solely a theoretical concept, but rather a practical and iterative process that requires active participation and experimentation.

Experimental Iteration

Experimental Iteration is a core principle within Design Thinking disciplines that involves the process of iteratively refining and improving a design through multiple rounds of testing and evaluation. It emphasizes the importance of learning from failures, recognizing that each iteration of the design provides valuable insights and opportunities for improvement.

The process of Experimental Iteration typically begins with the creation of a prototype or initial design concept. This prototype is then tested with users or stakeholders in order to gather feedback and identify areas for improvement. By involving users early on in the design process, designers are able to gain a deeper understanding of their needs and preferences, ultimately leading to a more user-centered design.

Based on the feedback received, designers then make iterative changes to the design, addressing the identified areas for improvement. This process is repeated multiple times, with each iteration building upon the previous one. Each round of testing and evaluation provides designers with new insights and learnings, allowing them to refine and enhance the design as they progress.

41

Experimental Iteration is an essential component of Design Thinking as it encourages designers to embrace a mindset of continuous learning and improvement. By actively seeking feedback, designers are able to create designs that are more aligned with user needs and expectations, resulting in better overall experiences. Through the iterative process of Experimental Iteration, designers are able to take calculated risks, test assumptions, and make evidence-based decisions, ultimately leading to more innovative and successful outcomes.

Experimental Iterations

Experimental iterations refer to the repetitive process of testing and iterating a design solution through experimentation. It is a key component of the Design Thinking discipline, which is a problem-solving approach that aims to understand and address people's needs and desires.

In the context of Design Thinking, experimental iterations involve creating prototypes or mock-ups of a design solution and then testing it with users or stakeholders to gather feedback and insights. These prototypes can be physical or digital representations of the design, ranging from simple sketches to interactive models. Through these experiments, designers can uncover what works and what doesn't, and make informed adjustments and refinements to improve the solution.

Experimental Learning

Experimental learning refers to the process of acquiring knowledge and skills through hands-on experiences, active experimentation, and reflection. It is a central component of Design Thinking, a problem-solving approach that emphasizes empathy, creativity, and iteratively refining solutions.

In the context of Design Thinking, experimental learning involves actively engaging with the problem or challenge at hand, rather than relying solely on theoretical knowledge or passive observation. It encourages designers to generate ideas, prototype solutions, and test them in real-world situations to gather valuable feedback and insights.

This approach recognizes that failure is an essential part of the learning process. Designers actively embrace setbacks and use them as opportunities for growth and improvement. By experimenting and iterating, designers can uncover new possibilities, challenge assumptions, and uncover unexpected insights that lead to innovative solutions.

At its core, experimental learning in Design Thinking is rooted in a human-centered approach. It involves interacting with users, stakeholders, and the broader context to understand their needs, uncover hidden motivations, and gain a deep understanding of the problem space. This empathetic understanding allows designers to create solutions that truly address user needs and provide meaningful experiences.

Feature Driven Development (FDD)

Feature Driven Development (FDD) is an iterative and incremental software development framework that is consistent with Agile principles and methodologies. It is primarily used in project management disciplines to provide a structured approach for delivering high-quality software products efficiently.

In FDD, the software development process is organized around a set of features or functionalities that need to be implemented. These features are identified by the project stakeholders and are prioritized based on their importance and business value. Each feature is broken down into smaller, more manageable tasks and assigned to individual developers or development teams.

The development process in FDD consists of five key activities: developing an overall model, building a feature list, planning by feature, design by feature, and building by feature. The overall model provides an abstract representation of the system and helps in identifying the key domain classes and their relationships. The feature list is created by breaking down the system into a set of features that can be implemented independently. Planning by feature involves creating plans for each feature, including estimation of efforts and scheduling. Design by feature focuses

42

on designing individual features and their component classes. Building by feature involves coding, testing, integrating, and delivering each feature incrementally.

FDD emphasizes on a strong project management approach to ensure smooth and efficient development. It encourages regular and effective communication among the development teams and stakeholders. FDD places emphasis on code ownership and collective code ownership, promoting collaborative and team-oriented development.

Feature Flag

A feature flag is a method used in Agile Process and Project Management disciplines to control and manage the release of new features or changes in software development projects. It is a way to introduce flexibility and control into the development process by allowing teams to toggle features on and off without the need for deploying new code or making significant changes to the existing codebase.

With feature flags, different functionalities can be enabled or disabled dynamically, depending on the desired behavior or user segment. This provides the ability to test new features with a controlled group of users, gather feedback, and make adjustments before fully rolling them out to all users. This incremental approach allows for faster and more efficient development as it reduces the risk and impact of introducing new features or changes to the system.

Feature Injection

Feature Injection is a technique used in the Agile Process and Project Management disciplines to identify and prioritize features in a software project. It involves understanding the needs and goals of the stakeholders and incorporating those into the project design.

During the feature injection process, a collaborative approach is taken to gather requirements and prioritize them based on their value to the end users. This technique promotes effective communication between the development team and the stakeholders, ensuring that everyone is aligned with the project objectives.

The process starts by identifying the primary goal of the project and the features that are essential to achieve that goal. The development team then works closely with the stakeholders to gather user stories, scenarios, and examples that further define these features.

Once the key features are identified, they are prioritized based on their value to the stakeholders. This prioritization is done using techniques such as MoSCoW (Must, Should, Could, Won't) or Value versus Effort analysis.

Feature Injection also involves breaking down the identified features into smaller, manageable tasks or user stories. This helps in organizing the development process and improving the overall efficiency of the team.

By using Feature Injection, Agile teams are able to ensure that the project features align with the goals and needs of the stakeholders. This results in a more focused and successful development process, leading to higher customer satisfaction and value delivery.

Feature

The Agile Process refers to a project management approach that focuses on flexibility, collaboration, and adaptability. It emphasizes iterative and incremental development, allowing for continuous improvement and customer feedback throughout the project.

In Agile, projects are divided into small, manageable tasks called user stories, which are prioritized based on their value to the customer. These user stories are then assigned to cross-functional teams, typically consisting of developers, testers, and product owners, who work together to deliver working software in short, time-boxed iterations known as sprints.

One of the key principles of Agile is the ability to respond to change rather than strictly following a predefined plan. This means that requirements, priorities, and even project goals can be adjusted as needed to meet evolving customer needs and market conditions.

Agile also promotes close collaboration and communication among team members, as well as with stakeholders and customers. Daily stand-up meetings, regular demo sessions, and frequent feedback loops help ensure that everyone is aligned and that any issues or roadblocks are quickly addressed.

Agile project management techniques, such as Kanban or Scrum, provide frameworks and tools to support the Agile process. These methodologies provide a structured approach to planning, organizing, and tracking work, while still allowing for flexibility and adaptability.

In summary, Agile Process and Project Management disciplines are focused on delivering value to the customer through iterative development, continuous improvement, and close collaboration. It enables teams to quickly respond to changing requirements and deliver high-quality software in a flexible and adaptive manner.

Feedback Loop

A feedback loop in the context of Agile Process and Project Management disciplines refers to the iterative process of receiving and incorporating feedback throughout a project's duration.

In Agile methodologies, such as Scrum, feedback loops are essential for ensuring continuous improvement and adapting to changing requirements. The feedback loop typically consists of several steps:

1. Gathering feedback: This involves soliciting input from stakeholders, including team members, clients, and end-users. The feedback can come in various forms, such as verbal or written comments, surveys, or user testing results.

2. Analyzing feedback: Once feedback is collected, it is analyzed to understand its implications and identify areas for improvement. This step involves considering both positive and negative feedback and determining how best to address any concerns or suggestions.

3. Incorporating feedback: The next step is to incorporate the feedback into the project. This may involve revising project plans, adjusting priorities, or making changes to the product itself. The goal is to use the feedback to enhance the project's outcomes and meet the stakeholders' needs.

4. Reflecting and iterating: After incorporating the feedback, the team reflects on the changes made and assesses their impact. This reflection informs the team's future actions and iterations, allowing for continuous improvement throughout the project.

Feedback

Agile Process: Agile process refers to a project management approach that emphasizes flexibility and collaboration. It involves breaking a project into smaller increments called iterations, which are then executed in short timeframes known as sprints. The Agile process encourages continuous improvement and allows for changes and adjustments to be made throughout the project's lifecycle. This iterative approach promotes adaptive planning, early delivery of results, and frequent customer feedback. Agile teams work in a collaborative and self-organizing manner, prioritizing individuals and interactions over processes and tools. The Agile process can be applied to various domains, but it is particularly well-suited for software development projects.

Project Management: Project management is a discipline that involves planning, organizing, and controlling resources in order to achieve specific objectives within a defined timeframe. It encompasses the application of knowledge, skills, tools, and techniques to meet project requirements and ensure successful project completion. Project management involves the initiation, planning, execution, monitoring, and closing phases. It includes activities such as defining project scope, determining project objectives, identifying project stakeholders, developing a project schedule, allocating resources, managing risks, and monitoring progress. The role of a project manager is to lead and coordinate the project team, making sure that tasks are completed on time, within budget, and according to quality standards. Effective project management ensures that projects are delivered successfully, meeting stakeholder expectations and achieving the desired outcomes.

Flow Efficiency

Flow efficiency, in the context of Agile Process and Project Management disciplines, refers to the measure of how well work flows through a system or process with minimal delays and waste. It is a key metric used to assess the efficiency and effectiveness of a team or organization in delivering value to customers.

This concept is often associated with Lean principles, which aim to eliminate waste and optimize the flow of work. Flow efficiency focuses on the time spent on value-added activities versus the time spent on non-value-added activities, such as waiting, handoffs, and rework.

By analyzing flow efficiency, teams can identify and address bottlenecks, constraints, and factors that impede the smooth flow of work. This allows them to make data-driven decisions to improve overall productivity, throughput, and lead time.

Measuring flow efficiency involves collecting data on the time each task or work item spends in different stages of the process, such as backlog, in progress, and completed. By visualizing this data using tools like Kanban boards or value stream maps, teams can identify areas for improvement and implement strategies to increase flow efficiency.

Ultimately, the goal of focusing on flow efficiency is to deliver value to customers more quickly, predictably, and consistently, while minimizing waste and increasing overall team productivity.

Flow

The flow, in the context of Agile Process and Project Management disciplines, refers to the smooth and uninterrupted movement of work items through the various stages of the project. It emphasizes the importance of continuously delivering value to customers in a timely manner.

In Agile, flow is achieved through the use of different techniques and practices, such as visualizing the work, limiting work in progress, and applying feedback loops. Visualizing the work involves creating a visual representation, such as a Kanban board, to track and understand the status of each work item. Limiting work in progress ensures that the team focuses on completing a smaller number of tasks at a time, reducing multitasking and increasing overall efficiency.

Flow is closely related to the concept of cycle time, which measures the time it takes for a work item to move from start to finish. By monitoring and optimizing cycle time, teams can identify bottlenecks and areas for improvement in their process. Feedback loops, in the form of regular inspections and retrospectives, allow teams to reflect on their performance and make necessary adjustments to enhance the flow.

By promoting a steady flow, Agile frameworks enable teams to deliver value incrementally and iteratively, allowing for earlier and continuous feedback from stakeholders. This iterative approach enables the team to respond quickly to changes, adapt their plans, and deliver high-quality products.

Frequent Delivery

Frequent Delivery is a concept in Agile Process and Project Management disciplines that emphasizes the importance of regularly providing working software or deliverables to the stakeholders. It is a key principle of Agile methodologies such as Scrum, Kanban, and Extreme Programming (XP), where delivering value quickly and frequently is prioritized. In Agile Project Management, the focus is on breaking down the project into smaller, manageable pieces called iterations or sprints. Frequent Delivery ensures that at the end of each iteration, a potentially shippable product increment is delivered to the customer or stakeholder for feedback and validation. This iterative approach allows for the quick incorporation of feedback and changes, resulting in more accurate and relevant final deliverables. The benefits of Frequent Delivery are manifold. It promotes transparency, as stakeholders are regularly involved in the development process and can provide feedback early on. It also allows for early detection of risks and issues, enabling timely resolution. Regular delivery of working software also provides opportunities for validation and testing, reducing the chances of defects or bugs being carried forward. By continually delivering increments, the project team can align their efforts with evolving stakeholder requirements, adapt to changes in priorities, and ensure maximum value creation. Frequent Delivery also fosters a culture of continuous improvement, as the team can reflect on their progress, identify areas for enhancement, and make necessary adjustments. Overall, Frequent Delivery is a critical aspect of Agile Process and Project Management. It promotes collaboration, flexibility, and customer satisfaction by providing regular, tangible outputs throughout the project lifecycle.

Gamification Strategies

Gamification strategies refer to the implementation of game elements, mechanics, and dynamics in non-game contexts to engage and motivate users in achieving desired outcomes. It is a design thinking discipline that leverages the principles of game design to solve problems and enhance user experiences.

Incorporating gamification strategies involves identifying the target audience's motivations, designing meaningful challenges, and providing rewards and feedback to encourage desired behaviors. By tapping into people's natural inclination for play and competition, gamification can increase participation, foster learning, and drive desired actions.

Gamification

Gamification is a technique used in the context of Design Thinking disciplines to enhance user engagement and motivation by incorporating game elements and mechanics into non-game contexts. It involves applying game design principles, such as competition, rewards, challenges, and feedback loops, to non-game experiences to make them more enjoyable and interactive.

The goal of gamification is to tap into the intrinsic human desire for achievement, recognition, and competition, encouraging users to actively participate and adopt desired behaviors. By introducing game elements, such as points, levels, badges, and leaderboards, designers can create a sense of progress, status, and competition, which motivates users to engage more deeply with the experience.

Gamification can be implemented in various fields, including education, marketing, healthcare, and workplace environments. In education, gamification can make learning more engaging, encouraging students to actively participate and retain information. In marketing, it can be used to create interactive campaigns and reward customer loyalty. In healthcare, it can motivate individuals to adopt healthier habits and adhere to medical treatments. In the workplace, gamification can improve employee engagement, productivity, and collaboration.

However, it is crucial to balance the game elements with the overall user experience and the desired outcomes. Gamification should not overshadow the core purpose of the experience or become a mere gimmick. It should be strategically implemented to align with the users' goals, provide meaningful challenges, and offer relevant rewards and feedback. Successful gamification requires a deep understanding of the target audience, their motivations, and the context in which the experience is taking place.

Gamified Solutions

Gamified Solutions are design thinking disciplines that incorporate game elements and mechanics into non-game contexts, with the goal of engaging and motivating users to achieve specific objectives.

These solutions leverage the inherent characteristics of games, such as competition, rewards, challenges, and feedback, to enhance user experiences, drive desired behaviors, and solve problems effectively.

Hackathon

A hackathon is a time-bound, collaborative event where a group of individuals come together to solve a specific problem or develop a new product or service using Agile Process and Project Management disciplines. It is characterized by its intense, fast-paced nature and its focus on innovation, teamwork, and creativity.

During a hackathon, participants work in teams to brainstorm ideas, plan and execute projects, and develop prototypes or solutions within a set timeframe, often ranging from a few hours to a few days. They apply Agile Process and Project Management principles to ensure efficient and effective project delivery.

The Agile Process is a flexible and iterative approach to project management that emphasizes collaboration, adaptability, and continuous improvement. It is based on the Agile Manifesto and its twelve principles, which prioritize customer satisfaction, active stakeholder involvement, frequent product delivery, and embracing change. In the context of a hackathon, Agile Process allows teams to quickly respond to challenges, adjust project plans, and deliver tangible outcomes in a short period.

Meanwhile, Project Management disciplines provide a structured framework for organizing, planning, and executing projects. They encompass various techniques, methodologies, and tools to ensure project success, including project initiation, resource allocation, risk management, progress tracking, and communication. In a hackathon, the application of Project Management disciplines helps teams manage their time, resources, and deliverables effectively, ensuring that objectives are met within the given constraints.

Holistic Approach

A holistic approach in the context of Design Thinking disciplines refers to an inclusive and comprehensive approach that considers all aspects of a problem or situation in order to develop effective solutions. It involves examining the problem from multiple perspectives, understanding the underlying causes and interconnectedness of various factors, and considering the broader context in which the problem exists.

By adopting a holistic approach, designers are able to gain a deeper understanding of the problem and its root causes, which in turn allows them to generate more innovative and targeted solutions. This approach requires designers to go beyond surface-level observations and consider the social, cultural, economic, and environmental factors that impact the problem. It encourages interdisciplinary collaboration and engagement with stakeholders to ensure that all relevant perspectives are taken into account.

Holistic Design

Holistic design is a problem-solving approach within the realm of design thinking disciplines that aims to create comprehensive solutions by considering the entire ecosystem and context in which a problem exists, rather than focusing on individual components or isolated aspects. It embraces a holistic view of the problem, recognizing that all aspects are interconnected and interdependent, and seeks to design solutions that optimize the overall system rather than just its individual parts.

This approach requires a deep understanding of the problem space, including the needs, desires, behaviors, and constraints of all stakeholders involved. It involves gathering and synthesizing diverse perspectives, integrating various disciplines and domains of knowledge, and considering the environmental, social, economic, and cultural implications of design decisions.

Holistic Perspective

A holistic perspective in the context of design thinking disciplines refers to a comprehensive and integrated approach to problem-solving and innovation. It takes into account the interconnectedness and interdependencies of various factors and stakeholders involved in the design process.

Design thinking is a human-centered approach that emphasizes empathy, collaboration, and iterative problem-solving. A holistic perspective goes beyond considering individual components or elements of a design solution and instead takes a broader view of the entire system or ecosystem in which the design exists.

This perspective encourages designers to consider the context, environment, and larger social, cultural, and economic factors that may influence the success or effectiveness of a design solution. It involves a deep understanding of the needs, desires, and motivations of the end users or target audience, as well as the goals and objectives of the organization or stakeholders involved.

A holistic perspective also recognizes the importance of interdisciplinary collaboration and the integration of diverse perspectives and expertise. It encourages designers to work closely with individuals from different backgrounds, disciplines, and areas of expertise to gain insights, generate ideas, and test and refine design solutions.

By considering the holistic perspective, designers can create innovative and impactful solutions that address the underlying challenges and opportunities in a more comprehensive and sustainable way. It enables them to create designs that not only meet the functional requirements but also consider the broader social, environmental, and ethical implications.

Hypothesis-Driven Development

Hypothesis-Driven Development is a key concept in the Agile Process and Project Management disciplines. It refers to the practice of formulating and testing hypotheses during the development and implementation of a project. This approach is widely used in Agile methodologies such as Scrum, Lean, and Kanban to help teams deliver value and prioritize work effectively.

In Hypothesis-Driven Development, project teams start by identifying a specific problem or opportunity that they want to address. They then formulate a hypothesis, which is a proposed explanation or solution to the problem. This hypothesis is based on the team's current understanding and assumptions about the problem and the expected outcomes.

Once the hypothesis is defined, the team sets out to validate or invalidate it through experimentation and data analysis. They create small, time-boxed iterations or sprints to develop and test the necessary functionality. This iterative approach allows the team to gather feedback early and frequently from stakeholders and users, which helps to refine and adjust the hypothesis as new information emerges.

The main goal of Hypothesis-Driven Development is to reduce risk, increase learning, and drive innovation. By treating each hypothesis as an experiment, teams can gather empirical evidence to validate or invalidate their assumptions. This approach allows them to make data-driven decisions and adjust their project plans accordingly.

Hypothesis-Driven Development also enables teams to focus on the most valuable work, as they are constantly reassessing the hypothesis based on results and feedback. It encourages collaboration, transparency, and a culture of continuous learning and improvement.

Inclusive Problem Solving

Inclusive Problem Solving is a discipline within Design Thinking that emphasizes considering and addressing the needs, perspectives, and experiences of all individuals involved in the problem-solving process. It recognizes that diverse perspectives and inclusivity lead to more comprehensive and effective solutions.

This approach involves actively seeking out and involving people from different backgrounds, cultures, abilities, and experiences, as well as those who may be directly affected by the problem at hand. Inclusive Problem Solving aims to create a safe and respectful environment where everyone feels heard and valued.

Increment

Increment is a fundamental concept in Agile Process and Project Management disciplines. It refers to the iterative and incremental development approach in which a project is divided into small, manageable chunks called increments. Each increment represents a deliverable piece of work that adds value to the project and can be potentially released to users or stakeholders.

The concept of increment is closely tied to the Agile principle of delivering value early and continuously. By breaking the project into increments, teams can prioritize and focus on delivering the most valuable and critical features first, instead of trying to complete the entire project at once.

Incremental development allows for frequent feedback and validation from stakeholders, enabling teams to make adjustments and improvements throughout the project. It also promotes transparency and collaboration, as stakeholders can see tangible progress after each increment and provide input on future iterations.

Each increment builds upon the previous ones, gradually adding functionality and refinement to the project. This iterative approach allows teams to adapt to changing requirements, technology advancements, and user feedback, reducing the risk of building unnecessary or outdated features.

Furthermore, increments provide the opportunity for early and continuous testing, ensuring that quality is built into the project from the start. By testing each increment, teams can identify and address issues early on, making it easier to maintain and enhance the project over time.

Incremental Delivery

Incremental delivery is a fundamental concept in Agile Process and Project Management disciplines. It refers to the iterative and incremental development approach where the project or product is delivered in small, working increments rather than all at once. This approach enables the project team to deliver value to stakeholders on a regular basis, providing early and frequent opportunities for feedback and adaptation.

In an incremental delivery approach, the project is divided into manageable modules or features, with each increment being planned, developed, and tested separately. The development team focuses on delivering a working version of the product or module, ensuring that it is usable and provides value to the end-users. This allows for early validation of requirements, identification of potential issues, and incorporation of feedback into subsequent increments.

By delivering the product or project in increments, the Agile team can adapt to changing requirements, priorities, and market conditions more effectively. This approach enhances flexibility, as it allows for ongoing feedback and continuous improvement. The stakeholders have the opportunity to review and provide inputs at regular intervals, ensuring that the final product meets their expectations.

Incremental delivery also promotes risk management, as any issues or challenges can be identified and addressed early on. It enables the project team to tackle complex problems in a controlled manner, reducing the chances of catastrophic failures or costly rework. Furthermore, incremental delivery facilitates faster time to market, allowing the organization to realize value sooner.

Incremental Development

Incremental development is a software development approach within the Agile Process and Project Management disciplines. It involves breaking down the development of a software project into smaller, manageable increments or iterations, with each increment adding new functionality to the system.

This approach focuses on delivering a working product or feature within a short time frame, typically ranging from a few weeks to a few months. It allows for continuous feedback and collaboration between the development team and stakeholders, ensuring that the final product meets the evolving needs of the users.

49

Incremental Value

Incremental value, in the context of Agile Process and Project Management disciplines, refers to the continuous delivery of valuable, working products or features throughout the duration of a project. It is a fundamental principle in Agile methodologies and is based on the idea of iterative development.

With incremental value, projects are broken down into smaller, manageable iterations called sprints or iterations. Each iteration aims to deliver a working product or feature that adds value to the end user. This allows the project team to receive early feedback, make adjustments, and ensure that the delivered functionality meets the customer's expectations.

Information Architecture

Information Architecture, within the context of Design Thinking disciplines, refers to the practice of organizing and structuring information in a way that enables effective communication, intuitive navigation, and seamless user experience. It involves the deliberate planning and design of information systems, such as websites, applications, and digital interfaces, to ensure that users can easily find, understand, and interact with the information presented.

The goal of Information Architecture is to create logical and coherent structures that support the goals and needs of both users and organizations. It requires a deep understanding of user behaviors, goals, and mental models, as well as a thorough analysis of the content and information to be organized. By strategically arranging and labeling information, information architects aim to reduce cognitive load, minimize confusion, and enhance overall usability.

Information Radiator

An Information Radiator is a visual display used in Agile Process and Project Management disciplines to provide real-time and easily digestible updates on project progress, performance, and relevant information. It acts as a communication tool, promoting transparency and collaboration among team members, stakeholders, and other interested parties.

In an Agile environment, where frequent iterations and quick decision-making are crucial, an Information Radiator serves as a central source of project-related data. It communicates important information at a glance, eliminating the need for individuals to seek out and compile updates manually.

Informed Risk-Taking

Informed risk-taking in the context of Design Thinking disciplines refers to the intentional and calculated act of pursuing innovative ideas with an awareness of potential uncertainties and challenges, supported by a thorough understanding of the problem space and user needs. It involves stepping outside of the comfort zone and taking calculated risks to explore new possibilities and push boundaries in the design process.

Design Thinking encourages practitioners to embrace ambiguity and view failure as a learning opportunity. Informed risk-taking requires a deep understanding of the problem and the intended users, gained through research and empathy-building activities. By thoroughly understanding the problem space, designers can identify and assess the potential risks associated with their concepts, ensuring they make informed decisions and mitigate potential negative consequences.

Additionally, informed risk-taking involves prototyping and testing ideas early and often. By creating low-fidelity prototypes and gathering feedback from users, designers can validate and refine their concepts continuously, reducing the risk of investing time, resources, and effort into ideas that may not resonate with users.

Incorporating informed risk-taking into the Design Thinking process encourages creativity and innovation while maintaining a level of practicality and feasibility. It allows designers to explore unconventional ideas, challenge assumptions, and discover unexpected solutions that can lead to breakthrough innovations.

Innovation Catalyst

An Innovation Catalyst is an individual or a team that drives and facilitates innovation within an organization or community by using Design Thinking disciplines.

Design Thinking is a human-centered approach to problem-solving that encourages creative and innovative solutions. It involves empathizing with users, defining their needs, ideating potential solutions, prototyping and testing those solutions, and ultimately implementing the most effective ones.

Innovation Catalysts

Innovation Catalysts are individuals or teams who are responsible for initiating and driving innovation within an organization using the principles and practices of Design Thinking. They act as the catalysts for change, fostering a culture of innovation and pushing the boundaries of what is possible.

These catalysts play a crucial role in the design thinking process by inspiring and empowering others to think creatively, encouraging collaboration, and facilitating the exploration of new ideas. They bring together diverse perspectives, skills, and expertise to tackle complex challenges and create innovative solutions that meet the needs of users and customers.

Innovation Culture

Innovation Culture refers to the environment, mindset, and practices that foster creativity, collaboration, and continuous improvement within an organization. It is a key component of Design Thinking disciplines, which aim to solve complex problems and drive innovation through a human-centered approach.

An innovation culture encourages individuals to think outside the box, challenge existing norms, and embrace a growth mindset. It values experimentation, risk-taking, and learning from failure as essential parts of the innovation process. In such a culture, individuals are empowered to share their ideas and insights openly, collaborate with others across different disciplines, and engage in iterative and user-centric design processes.

Innovation culture promotes cross-functional collaboration and breaks down silos that often hinder creativity and innovation. It encourages diverse perspectives and interdisciplinary teamwork, emphasizing the importance of empathy and understanding the needs and desires of end-users. By incorporating the principles of design thinking, organizations can create a culture where empathy, creativity, and experimentation thrive.

Furthermore, an innovation culture values continuous improvement and recognizes that innovation is a journey rather than a destination. It promotes a cycle of ideation, prototyping, testing, and iteration, with a strong focus on listening to user feedback and continuously refining solutions. This iterative approach allows organizations to stay adaptable and responsive in an ever-changing market.

In conclusion, innovation culture is a vital element of Design Thinking disciplines that nurtures creativity, collaboration, and continuous learning, enabling organizations to drive meaningful and impactful innovation.

Innovation Dashboards

Innovation Dashboards in the context of Design Thinking disciplines refer to visual tools or platforms that provide a holistic overview of an organization's innovation initiatives, progress, and outcomes. These dashboards are designed to capture and present data related to various aspects of the innovation process, such as ideation, prototyping, testing, and implementation.

The primary purpose of Innovation Dashboards is to help teams and stakeholders track and manage their innovation efforts effectively. They offer a consolidated view of key metrics, performance indicators, and qualitative insights, allowing users to make data-driven decisions and gauge the success of their innovation strategies.

Innovation Ecosystem

An innovation ecosystem refers to a collaborative network that fosters and supports the development of innovative ideas and solutions. It encompasses various stakeholders, including individuals, organizations, and institutions, all working together to create and implement new concepts.

Design thinking, as a discipline within the innovation ecosystem, emphasizes a human-centered approach to problem-solving. It involves empathizing with users, defining the core problem, ideating multiple solutions, prototyping, testing, and iterating to arrive at a desirable, feasible, and viable solution.

Innovation Games

Innovation Games are a set of collaborative activities and techniques used within Agile process and project management disciplines to elicit insights, capture ideas, and prioritize requirements from stakeholders. These games leverage the principles of game theory and gamification to encourage active participation, promote creativity, and drive innovation.

By engaging participants in structured gameplay, Innovation Games provide a fun and interactive way to gather information, gather diverse perspectives, and build shared understanding among team members and stakeholders. They enable teams to tap into the collective intelligence and wisdom of the group, fostering collaboration and driving decision-making that is based on evidence and insights rather than assumptions or personal opinions.

These games can be used at different stages throughout the Agile project lifecycle, from initial visioning and ideation to user story prioritization and validation. Some common examples of Innovation Games include "Prune the Product Tree," where participants collaboratively assess and prioritize product features, and "Buy a Feature," where participants use a limited budget to "purchase" features based on their perceived value.

Overall, Innovation Games serve as powerful tools for Agile teams and project managers to facilitate effective communication, increase stakeholder engagement, and ultimately deliver products and solutions that meet the needs and expectations of end-users.

Innovation

In the context of Agile Process and Project Management disciplines, innovation refers to the process of introducing new ideas, methods, or solutions to improve processes, products, or services in a continuously evolving and iterative manner.

Innovation within the Agile framework involves adopting a mindset that encourages experimentation, collaboration, and open communication. It promotes a culture of adaptability and flexibility, allowing teams to respond quickly to changing requirements or customer needs.

Innovative Solutions

Innovative Solutions refer to unique and creative ways of addressing complex problems or challenges through a Design Thinking approach. Design Thinking is a human-centered problem-solving methodology that focuses on understanding the needs and wants of the end-users to develop innovative solutions.

This approach involves five key stages: Empathize, Define, Ideate, Prototype, and Test. During the Empathize stage, designers immerse themselves in the users' context to gain a deep understanding of their needs, challenges, and aspirations. This helps to uncover insights and define the problem statement during the Define stage.

In the Ideate stage, designers generate a wide range of ideas, encouraging wild and unconventional thinking. These ideas are then consolidated and refined into concepts to be prototyped during the Prototype stage. Prototypes are low-fi representations of the potential solution that allow designers to gather feedback and further refine their ideas.

The final stage is Test, where prototypes are tested with the end-users, evaluating the feasibility, desirability, and viability of the solutions. The feedback from the testing phase informs potential iterations of the prototypes until a feasible and user-centric solution is achieved.

Innovative Solutions, driven by Design Thinking, aim to create meaningful and impactful solutions that address user needs while also considering the viability and sustainability of the solution. By prioritizing the customers and their experiences, Design Thinking enables the development of innovative solutions that have the potential to shape industries, improve processes, and positively impact society as a whole.

Insight Generation

Insight generation is a crucial step in the Design Thinking process, which involves the gathering and synthesis of information to uncover deep-rooted understanding and identify opportunities for innovation. It aims to develop a comprehensive understanding of the problem or challenge at hand by gaining insights into the needs, desires, behaviors, and motivations of the target audience or users.

During insight generation, designers employ various qualitative research methods such as in-depth interviews, observations, and empathy-building activities to immerse themselves in the users' context. These methods help them to capture first-hand experiences and gather valuable data that goes beyond surface-level observations. Designers also utilize tools like affinity diagrams and journey mapping to organize and visualize the collected information, enabling them to identify patterns, establish connections, and derive meaningful insights.

By deeply understanding the users' pain points, aspirations, and motivations, designers can uncover latent needs and unmet desires. These insights provide a fresh perspective and the foundation for ideation, prototyping, and further exploration. They enable designers to empathize with the users, challenge assumptions, and generate innovative ideas that address the identified problems or opportunities.

In summary, insight generation in the context of Design Thinking is the process of gathering and synthesizing information to develop a holistic understanding of users' needs, desires, behaviors, and motivations. It involves qualitative research methods, data visualization techniques, and deep empathy-building activities to uncover valuable insights that drive innovation and problem-solving in the design process.

Insightful Discoveries

Insightful discoveries are significant findings or revelations made during the process of applying design thinking disciplines. Design thinking, a problem-solving approach that emphasizes empathy, creativity, and iterative prototyping, aims to uncover user needs and create innovative solutions.

In the context of design thinking, insightful discoveries refer to the unique and profound insights gained through various methods, such as user research, observation, and interviews. These discoveries can be unexpected or counterintuitive, revealing hidden user behaviors, pain points, desires, or motivations. They help designers and teams gain a deeper understanding of the problem at hand and serve as the foundation for generating creative and effective solutions.

Insightful Discovery

Insightful Discovery refers to a critical phase in the Design Thinking process where designers seek to gain a deep understanding of the problem or challenge at hand. It involves going beyond surface-level observations and delving into the underlying needs, motivations, and emotions of the users or stakeholders involved. This phase is often characterized by extensive research, empathy-building activities, and the analysis of gathered data to uncover valuable insights.

During the Insightful Discovery phase, designers employ various techniques such as conducting interviews, observations, and surveys to gather qualitative and quantitative data. They aim to empathize with the target audience and gain a comprehensive understanding of their experiences, pain points, and aspirations related to the problem area. This helps designers develop a nuanced perspective and uncover insights that can inform the subsequent stages of the design process.

Inspect And Adapt

Inspect and Adapt is a crucial concept within the Agile Process and Project Management disciplines. It refers to the continuous evaluation and adjustment of processes and practices in response to feedback and changing circumstances. This iterative approach allows teams to improve their performance and deliver better value to customers.

In the Agile context, Inspect and Adapt involves regularly reviewing the progress and outcomes of a project and making necessary adjustments. This is done through various activities such as retrospectives, reviews, and demonstrations. The purpose is to identify what is working well, what needs improvement, and what changes can be made to enhance the team's effectiveness.

Inspection

Inspection is a formal process that is an integral part of Agile Process and Project Management disciplines. It involves carefully reviewing and examining various aspects of a project or process to identify any potential issues, errors, or opportunities for improvement. The primary objective of an inspection is to ensure that the project or process meets the desired standards and requirements.

During an inspection, a team of relevant stakeholders, including developers, testers, business analysts, and project managers, come together to thoroughly assess and evaluate the project or process. They closely examine all relevant documentation, code, designs, and other artifacts in order to identify any deviations from the defined standards or any potential risks.

The inspection process typically follows a structured approach, where a checklist or set of predefined criteria is used to guide the evaluation. This helps ensure consistency and thoroughness in the inspection process. The team members provide their observations, suggestions, and recommendations based on their expertise and experience.

Once the inspection is complete, the findings are documented and shared with the relevant stakeholders. This includes identifying any deviations, errors, or areas for improvement, as well as proposing corrective actions or suggestions to address them. The team then collaboratively decides on the appropriate course of action, which may involve making necessary changes to the project or process.

Overall, inspection plays a critical role in Agile Process and Project Management disciplines by providing a formal mechanism for identifying and addressing potential issues or risks. It helps ensure the quality, consistency, and adherence to standards in projects and processes, leading to successful outcomes.

Interdisciplinary Collaboration

Interdisciplinary collaboration in the context of Design Thinking disciplines refers to the seamless integration and collaboration between individuals from diverse fields, such as design, technology, psychology, business, and engineering, to create innovative solutions to complex problems.

Through interdisciplinary collaboration, experts from different disciplines bring their unique perspectives, knowledge, and skills to the table, allowing for a holistic approach to problem-solving. This diversity of expertise facilitates the exploration of different angles and possibilities, leading to more comprehensive, creative, and effective solutions.

Interdisciplinary Solutions

Interdisciplinary Solutions refer to the collaborative approach of solving complex problems by integrating knowledge and expertise from multiple fields within the context of Design Thinking disciplines. It involves bringing together professionals from diverse backgrounds, such as designers, engineers, psychologists, and sociologists, to work together and leverage their unique perspectives in order to develop innovative solutions.

By incorporating interdisciplinary teams and methods into the Design Thinking process, organizations can benefit from a broader range of insights and approaches. This allows for more holistic problem-solving, as complex challenges often require a multidimensional understanding and consideration of various factors. Interdisciplinary Solutions encourage cross-pollination of ideas and facilitate creative thinking, leading to transformative and effective outcomes.

Intuition

Intuition, within the context of Design Thinking disciplines, is the ability to understand and solve problems based on instinctive gut feelings rather than solely relying on analysis and logic. It is an innate knowledge that individuals possess, allowing them to make quick and effective decisions based on their previous experiences and insights.

This intuitive approach is crucial in Design Thinking as it enables designers to tap into their creativity, empathy, and interdisciplinary perspectives. By relying on their intuition, designers can uncover unique and innovative solutions that may not have been evident through traditional problem-solving methods.

Iteration Planning

An iteration planning is a crucial aspect of the Agile process and project management disciplines. It involves the process of deciding which user stories, tasks, and features will be included in the upcoming iteration or sprint. The aim is to create a plan that maximizes the value delivered to the customer while minimizing risks and uncertainties.

During the iteration planning, the team collaborates to identify and prioritize the most important user stories or product backlog items (PBIs) that will be worked on in the next iteration. The team reviews the list of PBIs, breaks them down into smaller tasks or sub-tasks, and estimates the effort required to complete them.

Once the user stories and tasks are identified, the team determines the order in which they will be worked on based on their priority and dependencies. The team also considers their capacity and velocity to ensure a realistic plan is created. The iteration planning involves a collaborative effort, with input from the entire team, including developers, testers, and other stakeholders.

The outcome of iteration planning is a clear plan that outlines the scope for the upcoming iteration, the tasks and user stories that will be worked on, and the estimated effort required for each. This plan serves as a guide for the team throughout the iteration, helping them stay focused, track progress, and deliver value incrementally.

Iteration Zero

Iteration Zero is an initial phase in the Agile Process and Project Management disciplines. It marks the beginning of a project, where the team lays the foundation for a successful Agile development process. During this phase, the team focuses on setting up an environment that fosters effective collaboration, communication, and planning.

The primary goal of Iteration Zero is to establish a clear understanding of the project scope, objectives, and constraints. It involves gathering requirements and creating a product roadmap that outlines the high-level features and deliverables. This helps in aligning the team's vision and goals, ensuring everyone is on the same page before commencing the development process.

Additionally, Iteration Zero focuses on the preparation and arrangement of necessary resources and infrastructure. This may include setting up development environments, configuring tools and frameworks, and establishing communication channels. The team also identifies any external dependencies or constraints that could potentially impact the project timeline or progress.

Moreover, Iteration Zero emphasizes creating a cooperative team culture by fostering open communication and trust among team members. It encourages the establishment of Agile practices, such as daily stand-up meetings, grooming sessions, and iteration planning meetings.

These practices enhance transparency, collaboration, and continuous improvement throughout the project.

Iteration

An iteration, in the context of Agile Process and Project Management disciplines, refers to a time-bound, recurring cycle or phase within a development project. It is a fundamental part of Agile methodologies, such as Scrum, that emphasize iterative and incremental development.

During an iteration, a defined set of tasks, features, or user stories are completed in a timeboxed period, known as a sprint. The length of an iteration can vary depending on the project's needs and team dynamics, but typically ranges from one to four weeks. At the end of each iteration, there is a tangible deliverable, which is a working product that can be tested, evaluated, and potentially released.

Iterative Development

Iterative development is a fundamental concept within the Agile Process and Project Management disciplines. It involves breaking down a large project or task into smaller, more manageable iterations or cycles. Each iteration focuses on delivering a working product or feature that adds value to the customer or end user.

During each iteration, a cross-functional team collaborates together to plan and execute the work necessary to achieve the iteration's goals. They prioritize the tasks and allocate resources accordingly, ensuring that the most valuable and high-priority work is completed first. This approach allows for the continuous delivery of incremental improvements or features, providing immediate feedback and value to the customer.

At the end of each iteration, the team reviews and reflects on the work completed, assessing what went well and what can be improved. This feedback loop allows for continuous learning and adaptation, which is a core principle of the Agile Process. The team then uses this feedback to inform their planning and execution in subsequent iterations, making necessary adjustments and refinements to improve the overall project or product.

Iterative development promotes flexibility and adaptability, as it recognizes that requirements and priorities may change over time. By delivering working increments of the project on a regular basis, it allows for earlier validation of assumptions and encourages collaboration and communication between stakeholders.

Overall, iterative development is a key component of the Agile Process and Project Management disciplines. It enables teams to consistently deliver value, learn from their experiences, and adapt to changing circumstances, ultimately leading to the successful completion of projects that meet the needs and expectations of the customer.

Iterative Process

An iterative process refers to a cyclic approach of development and improvement that is commonly used in the Agile Process and Project Management disciplines. It involves breaking down a large project into smaller increments or iterations, where each iteration consists of defined tasks and goals.

The iterative process follows a systematic approach where it focuses on continuously refining and enhancing the project based on feedback and lessons learned from each iteration. It allows for flexibility and adaptability, as changes can be made to the project during each iteration based on evolving requirements and stakeholder input.

Within the Agile Process, the iterative approach is fundamental to practices like Scrum and Kanban. In Scrum, iterations are called sprints, typically lasting from one to four weeks. At the end of each sprint, the team reviews the completed work and adapts the project plan for the next iteration. This approach allows for frequent inspection and adaptation, ensuring that the project is always aligned with the stakeholder's needs.

Similarly, in Project Management, the iterative process is used to manage projects with changing requirements. It acknowledges that not all project details can be known upfront and that modifications may be necessary during the development cycle. By breaking the project into smaller iterations, project managers can regularly assess progress, identify potential risks, and make adjustments to deliver a high-quality project.

Joint Application Development (JAD)

Joint Application Development (JAD) is a collaborative approach used in Agile Process and Project Management disciplines to facilitate communication and collaboration between stakeholders, developers, and project teams. JAD aims to gather requirements and define project goals through interactive sessions and workshops.

In the context of Agile Process, JAD is particularly beneficial as it promotes close collaboration and transparency between all key stakeholders. It enables the project team to quickly and iteratively gather requirements, gain a deep understanding of user needs, and prioritize features in an agile and adaptive manner.

During JAD sessions, stakeholders actively participate in discussions, brainstorming, and decision-making. This promotes a shared understanding of project goals, scope, and priorities, helping to set clear and achievable objectives. By involving stakeholders early in the development process, JAD minimizes the risk of miscommunication and misunderstandings, which can lead to costly rework and delays.

JAD sessions typically involve workshops, interviews, and brainstorming sessions. During these sessions, stakeholders and developers work together to identify requirements, outline system architecture, and design solutions. Visual aids such as diagrams, flowcharts, and mockups are often used to enhance understanding and facilitate communication.

The use of JAD in Agile Project Management facilitates a high degree of stakeholder involvement, collaboration, and transparency, fostering a sense of ownership and commitment to project success. JAD ensures that the final product meets the needs and expectations of all stakeholders, minimizing the potential for scope creep and increasing the overall efficiency and effectiveness of the development process.

Just-In-Time

Just-In-Time (JIT) is a methodology commonly used in Agile Process and Project Management disciplines. It is a production strategy designed to maintain efficiency by producing and delivering work items or deliverables precisely when they are needed, and not before. JIT is based on the premise that unnecessary accumulation of work items or deliverables leads to waste and inefficiency.

In the context of Agile Process and Project Management, JIT emphasizes the importance of delivering value to the customer in small, frequent increments. It encourages teams to work on and complete only those work items or deliverables that are immediately required and prioritized by the customer or product owner. This approach aims to eliminate unnecessary work and decrease the time spent on tasks that do not directly contribute to the end result.

JIT helps to optimize the flow of work, reduce lead times, and enhance flexibility. By focusing on delivering valuable features or functionality in a timely manner, JIT enables project teams to quickly adapt to changing requirements and customer feedback. It minimizes the risk of building unnecessary features or wasting effort on work that may become obsolete or irrelevant as project priorities evolve.

In summary, Just-In-Time is a concept within Agile Process and Project Management that advocates for the timely delivery of work items or deliverables based on immediate customer needs. It aims to minimize waste, optimize efficiency, and improve adaptability by prioritizing and completing only the most valuable tasks at any given time.

Kaikaku

Kaikaku is a Japanese term which translates to "radical change" or "reform" in English. In the context of Agile Process and Project Management disciplines, Kaikaku refers to a proactive and revolutionary approach to change within an organization. It involves implementing large-scale transformative measures to achieve significant improvements in process efficiency, performance, and outcomes.

A key characteristic of Kaikaku is its disruptive nature, as it challenges traditional ways of thinking and operating. By going beyond incremental improvements, Kaikaku aims to initiate rapid and substantial changes that can lead to breakthrough results. It involves questioning existing practices, identifying bottlenecks and inefficiencies, and introducing radical interventions to eliminate waste and optimize performance.

Kaizen

Kaizen, in the context of Agile Process and Project Management disciplines, refers to a continuous improvement approach that focuses on making incremental changes to processes, products, and services.

Derived from the Japanese words "kai" (which means change) and "zen" (which means good), Kaizen embodies the philosophy of constantly striving for improvement. It is a key principle in the Agile methodology, which emphasizes adaptability, collaboration, and frequent iterations.

Kanban Board

A Kanban Board is a visual project management tool that is used in Agile processes to help teams manage their work more effectively. It provides a clear and straightforward way for team members to see what work needs to be done, what is currently in progress, and what work has been completed.

The board is usually divided into columns that represent different stages of the project, such as "To Do," "In Progress," and "Done." Each task or user story is represented by a card, which can be moved from one column to another as it progresses through the project. This allows team members to easily track the status of each task and prioritize their work accordingly.

Kanban

Kanban is a project management and workflow management system used within the Agile framework. It provides a visual representation of work items and tasks, allowing teams to visualize, track, and manage their work effectively.

The core concept of Kanban is to limit work in progress (WIP) to maintain a steady and balanced workflow. It is based on the principles of reducing waste, improving efficiency, and fostering continuous improvement.

Lateral Thinking

Lateral thinking is a problem-solving approach used in Agile Process and Project Management disciplines. It involves thinking outside the box and looking at the problem from different perspectives to generate innovative solutions.

In the context of Agile, which emphasizes adaptability and creativity, lateral thinking plays a crucial role in continuously improving processes and enhancing project outcomes. It challenges the traditional linear thinking and encourages team members to explore unconventional ideas and approaches.

Lead Time

Lead time in the context of Agile Process and Project Management refers to the time taken to complete a specific task or deliver a product or service from the point of initiation until it is ready for use or delivery. It is a measure of the elapsed time between the start of a process or activity and its completion.

In Agile methodologies, lead time is an important metric that helps teams track productivity and efficiency. It provides valuable insights into the overall performance of the team and can be used to identify bottlenecks or areas of improvement in the project workflow. Monitoring lead time allows teams to make data-driven decisions, prioritize work, and make necessary adjustments to meet project goals and deadlines.

Lean Startup

The Lean Startup is a methodology that applies the principles of Agile to the process of managing and developing projects. It is a systematic approach to creating and running startups, with a focus on continuous improvement and iteration. The Lean Startup philosophy centers around the idea of building a minimum viable product (MVP) and gathering feedback from customers early on in the development process. This feedback is used to inform subsequent iterations and improvements.

In the context of Agile Process and Project Management disciplines, the Lean Startup methodology promotes a mindset of learning and adaptation. It encourages teams to start small and quickly build, test, and validate ideas. By following a build-measure-learn feedback loop, teams can gather data on customer behavior and preferences, and make informed decisions based on this data. This iterative approach allows startups to avoid wasting resources on unnecessary features or products that do not meet customer needs.

Lean Thinking

Lean Thinking is a methodology and mindset rooted in the principles of continuous improvement, waste reduction, and value creation. It has gained significant prominence in the Agile Process and Project Management disciplines due to its focus on delivering high-quality products and services efficiently.

In the context of Agile Process and Project Management, Lean Thinking emphasizes optimizing workflows, streamlining processes, and eliminating waste. It encourages teams to constantly analyze and improve their practices to deliver more value to customers while minimizing non-value-added activities.

By adopting Lean Thinking, Agile teams strive to understand and prioritize customer needs, ensuring that the solutions they deliver are aligned with those needs. This involves fostering strong collaboration and communication across team members, stakeholders, and customers to identify and address potential bottlenecks, quality issues, or any other factors hindering value creation.

Additionally, Lean Thinking encourages the use of data-driven decision-making, leveraging metrics and continuous feedback loops to drive improvements. Agile teams apply Lean principles such as "just-in-time" delivery, reducing inventory and work in progress, and focusing on delivering the highest priority features with the least amount of effort.

Overall, Lean Thinking complements Agile Process and Project Management by promoting a culture of continuous improvement, waste reduction, and value-driven practices. It enables teams to create highly efficient workflows, enhance customer satisfaction, and achieve business goals while maintaining adaptability and responsiveness.

Lean

Lean in the context of Agile Process and Project Management disciplines refers to a methodology based on the principles of Lean Manufacturing, originally developed by Toyota. It focuses on maximizing customer value while minimizing waste and continuously improving processes.

In Lean, the key objective is to create a streamlined and efficient workflow that delivers high-quality products or services to the customer as quickly as possible. Waste is identified as anything that does not add value to the customer, such as waiting, unnecessary duplication, defects, overproduction, or excessive inventory.

The Lean methodology encourages cross-functional collaboration and empowers teams to make informed decisions. Daily stand-up meetings, known as "huddles," are held to ensure transparency and identify any obstacles or bottlenecks that may arise during the project.

Continuous improvement is a fundamental principle of Lean. Through regular retrospectives, the team reflects on their processes and identifies areas for improvement. This feedback loop enables incremental enhancements to the project delivery, resulting in increased efficiency and customer satisfaction.

Lean also promotes a culture of respect for people. Team members are empowered to voice their opinions, and collaboration is highly valued. This fosters a supportive and innovative environment that encourages learning and growth.

Overall, Lean in Agile Process and Project Management disciplines is a systematic approach that focuses on delivering customer value, reducing waste, and continuously improving processes to achieve better outcomes.

Mind Mapping

Mind Mapping is a visual thinking tool widely used in the disciplines of Design Thinking to explore and organize ideas, concepts, and information.

It involves creating a hierarchical and interconnected structure of nodes, where each node represents a key idea or concept. The nodes are connected by lines or branches, indicating relationships or associations between them.

The main purpose of mind mapping in Design Thinking is to stimulate creativity, foster ideation, and facilitate a holistic understanding of complex problems or design challenges. By visually capturing and organizing thoughts and ideas, it enables designers to uncover patterns, identify insights, and generate innovative solutions.

Mind mapping allows for non-linear and associative thinking, encouraging the exploration of various perspectives and connections. It promotes the generation of multiple ideas and encourages collaboration and collective thinking by involving multiple stakeholders in the process.

This technique enhances the ability to generate, organize, and communicate ideas effectively. The visual representation of information in a mind map makes it easier to comprehend complex relationships and concepts, enabling designers to grasp the big picture while also focusing on details.

Mind maps can be created using pen and paper, whiteboards, or digital tools that offer flexible and dynamic features. The use of colors, symbols, and images further aids in the organization and visualization of ideas.

In summary, mind mapping in the context of Design Thinking is a powerful tool that supports designers in generating, organizing, and communicating ideas. It fosters creativity, facilitates holistic understanding, and encourages collaboration by visualizing complex information in a structured and interconnected manner.

Mindful Exploration

Mindful exploration is a design thinking discipline that involves engaging in a deep and intentional examination of a problem or challenge. It is a process of analyzing and understanding the problem in order to generate innovative and effective solutions.

During mindful exploration, designers immerse themselves in the problem space, seeking to fully understand the needs and desires of the end-users or stakeholders. This involves conducting thorough research, collecting data, and gathering insights to gain a comprehensive understanding of the problem at hand.

The purpose of mindful exploration is to uncover hidden opportunities and potential solutions that may not be immediately apparent. By approaching the problem from different angles, designers are able to gain fresh perspectives and generate innovative ideas.

Through mindful exploration, designers are able to identify patterns, trends, and opportunities within the problem space. This helps them to gain a deeper understanding of the context in which the problem exists, and allows them to develop insights and make informed decisions.

Overall, mindful exploration is a critical step in the design thinking process as it lays the foundation for creating innovative and meaningful solutions. By taking the time to thoroughly explore and understand the problem, designers are able to develop empathetic and user-centered solutions that truly address the needs and desires of the end-users or stakeholders.

Mindful Innovation

Mindful Innovation is a concept within the discipline of Design Thinking that emphasizes the integration of mindfulness practices and principles into the innovation process. Design Thinking is a human-centered approach to problem-solving that seeks to understand and address the needs, desires, and experiences of the people for whom a product or service is being designed. Mindfulness, on the other hand, is a practice of paying attention to the present moment with non-judgmental awareness.

Mindful Innovation combines these two disciplines to create a more thoughtful and empathetic approach to the innovation process. It encourages designers and innovators to cultivate a state of mindfulness in order to fully understand and appreciate the nuances and complexities of the problems they are solving. By being present and aware, they can engage more deeply with the needs and desires of their users, uncovering insights and opportunities that may have been missed with a more traditional approach.

Mindful Observation

Mindful Observation is a practice utilized within the discipline of Design Thinking to deeply and intentionally observe, understand, and empathize with users, environments, and systems. It involves a systematic and conscious approach to immersing oneself in the context and intricacies of a situation, object, or problem, allowing for a holistic and unbiased understanding of the various elements and nuances at play.

During the process of Mindful Observation, designers and researchers engage their senses, thoughts, and emotions to gather rich and meaningful data. They focus on carefully observing and documenting details, behaviors, interactions, and patterns to uncover hidden insights and discover new possibilities. This practice encourages openness, curiosity, and non-judgment, enabling designers to step outside their own assumptions and preconceptions, and to truly understand the needs, desires, and challenges of users and stakeholders.

Minimum Marketable Feature (MMF)

Minimum Marketable Feature (MMF) is a concept used in Agile Process and Project Management disciplines to prioritize and deliver value to the customer in an incremental and iterative manner. It refers to a self-contained and independent piece of functionality that provides meaningful value to the user or customer and can be released or marketed independently.

MMFs are used to break down large and complex projects into smaller, manageable pieces that can be developed, tested, and released quickly. They are focused on delivering tangible benefits to the customer or end-user and are typically defined based on their marketability and capability to generate revenue or create a competitive advantage for the organization.

Minimum Viable Product (MVP)

A Minimum Viable Product (MVP) refers to the version of a product that has the minimum features necessary to satisfy the needs of early customers and gather feedback for future development. In the context of Agile Process and Project Management disciplines, an MVP is a strategy that prioritizes delivering the most value with the least effort and investment. It is a concept that allows teams to gather real user data and learn from it, while also reducing risk and optimizing resources.

By focusing on the core functionality and removing any additional features that are not essential for the initial release, an MVP allows teams to validate their product hypothesis and make faster iterations based on user feedback. The iterative nature of the Agile process enables teams to incrementally refine and enhance their product, incorporating user input and market demands into each iteration.

Mob Programming

Mob Programming is a development approach within the Agile process and project management disciplines that involves the participation of the entire team in collaborative software development. It is a means of achieving high-quality code, effective team collaboration, and increased productivity by bringing together multiple team members, often including developers, testers, analysts, and designers, to work together on a single task or piece of code.

In Mob Programming, the whole team actively engages in the development process, sharing their ideas, knowledge, and expertise to collectively solve problems, make decisions, and create software solutions. This approach promotes continuous learning, knowledge sharing, and collective ownership of the codebase. It helps ensure that all team members have a shared understanding of the project goals and requirements, as well as the technical details and challenges involved.

During a Mob Programming session, the team works together as a single entity, with one team member acting as the "driver" who actively writes code, while the other team members act as "navigators" who provide guidance, suggestions, and feedback. The roles of driver and navigators may rotate at regular intervals, allowing everyone to contribute actively and ensuring that different perspectives and ideas are considered.

Mob Programming not only enhances the quality of the code but also improves team dynamics, collaboration, and communication. It enables faster problem-solving, reduced bottlenecks, and increased efficiency by leveraging the collective intelligence, experience, and skills of the entire team. By working together in real-time, Mob Programming eliminates the need for handoffs, rework, and delays that can occur when tasks are divided among individual team members.

Muda

The term "muda" in the context of Agile Process and Project Management refers to the concept of waste. Originating from the Japanese word meaning "futility" or "uselessness," muda signifies any activity that does not add value to the final product or deliverable.

In Agile methodologies, such as Scrum or Kanban, muda is seen as an obstruction to efficiency and productivity. It is typically divided into three categories:

The first type of muda is known as "non-value-added activities." These are tasks that do not contribute to the final product or meet the customer's requirements. Examples include excessive documentation, unnecessary meetings, or redundant approvals. Agile teams seek to minimize or eliminate non-value-added activities to focus on delivering value to the customer.

The second type of muda is "process inefficiencies." This encompasses any bottlenecks, delays, or obstacles within the project management process. It can include waiting times, late feedback, or inadequate tools and resources. Agile teams aim to identify and address these inefficiencies promptly to maintain a smooth flow of work.

The third type of muda is "defects and rework." These refer to errors, bugs, or faults in the product or deliverable that require additional time and effort to fix or correct. Agile teams prioritize preventing defects by employing practices such as continuous integration and test-driven development.

The concept of muda encourages Agile teams to focus on eliminating waste and optimizing their processes. By doing so, teams can enhance productivity, deliver value to customers more efficiently, and achieve higher levels of overall quality in their work.

Nimble

Nimble is a term used in the context of Agile Process and Project Management disciplines. It refers to the ability of a team or organization to respond quickly and effectively to changes and challenges within a project.

In Agile methodologies, such as Scrum or Kanban, the focus is on iterative and incremental development, where requirements and solutions evolve through collaboration between self-organizing and cross-functional teams. Nimbleness is a key characteristic of these methodologies, as it allows teams to adapt to changing requirements, customer feedback, and market conditions.

No Estimates

No Estimates is a concept within the Agile Process and Project Management disciplines that challenges the traditional practice of providing time and effort estimates for completing tasks and delivering projects. It advocates for a more flexible and collaborative approach to planning and decision-making.

Avoiding estimates allows teams to focus on delivering value instead of getting tied up in lengthy estimation processes. By eliminating the need to estimate, teams can reduce waste, improve productivity, and increase customer satisfaction.

Obeya

Obeya is a concept used in Agile Process and Project Management disciplines that refers to a physical or virtual space where a cross-functional team gathers to visually track, plan, and communicate the progress of their work. The term "Obeya" is derived from Japanese, meaning "big room" or "war room," emphasizing the collaborative nature of the space.

In the context of Agile, an Obeya room serves as a central hub for the team, providing transparency and enabling constant communication and collaboration. It usually consists of large visual displays, such as whiteboards, charts, sticky notes, or digital tools, that represent the team's work and its progress. These visual aids help the team members to have a shared understanding of the project's status and foster open conversations about their work.

The Obeya room serves multiple purposes in Agile Project Management. Firstly, it enables teams to plan and organize their work by visualizing the tasks, backlog, and priorities. This visualization facilitates effective backlog management, sprint planning, and resource allocation. Secondly, the Obeya room acts as a communication tool, allowing team members to share information, discuss ideas, and resolve issues quickly. The visual displays encourage transparency, making it easier to identify dependencies, bottlenecks, and potential risks. Lastly, the Obeya room promotes continuous improvement by providing a dedicated space for retrospectives and feedback sessions, where the team can reflect on their processes, identify areas for improvement, and take actions accordingly.

Overhead

Overhead refers to any non-essential activities and resources that are required to support an Agile process or project management discipline. These activities and resources do not directly contribute to the value creation or delivery of the project, but they are necessary to enable and facilitate the efficient execution and control of the project.

In an Agile process, overhead includes activities such as planning, coordination, documentation, reporting, and meetings that are essential for project management but do not directly contribute to delivering the project's end product or features. The amount of overhead in an Agile process should be minimized to ensure that the focus remains on the delivery of customer value through working software.

Overhead in project management disciplines involves the allocation of resources and budget for activities that support the project, such as administrative tasks, communication, tracking, and quality assurance. This includes ensuring that the project has the necessary infrastructure, tools, and support systems in place to enable team collaboration and progress tracking.

Controlling overhead is crucial to ensure efficient project management and to minimize project costs and delays. Overhead activities should be streamlined, automated, and integrated whenever possible to reduce the time and effort required to perform them. The Agile principles of simplicity, self-organization, and continuous improvement should be applied to identify and eliminate unnecessary overhead, focusing on delivering the project's value with the least possible non-essential activities and resources.

Pair Design

Pair Design is a collaborative design approach where two designers work together in real-time to brainstorm, ideate, and create designs for a project. It is commonly used in Agile processes and Project Management disciplines to enhance creativity, improve the quality of design solutions, and promote knowledge sharing within a design team.

This design technique involves two team members, typically a designer and a developer, working together to tackle design challenges. They actively engage in discussions, ask each other questions, and provide immediate feedback on design decisions. By having two individuals involved in the design process, Pair Design encourages different perspectives and can lead to more innovative and well-rounded design solutions.

Pair Programming

Pair programming is a collaborative software development practice, commonly utilized in the Agile process and supported by Project Management disciplines. It involves two developers working together at a single workstation, actively collaborating and sharing responsibilities in the development process.

The developers, known as the "driver" and the "navigator," switch roles frequently. The driver focuses on the tactical aspects of writing code, while the navigator provides guidance, reviews, and suggests improvements. Through this constant collaboration, both participants are engaged in all aspects of the development, which leads to enhanced code quality, faster bug fixes, improved knowledge sharing, and increased team communication.

This practice brings numerous benefits to the Agile process and Project Management. It aids in reducing the chances of errors and defects, as potential issues are identified and addressed immediately. It also helps in promoting a cohesive and supportive team environment, enhancing team members' skills and fostering continuous learning. By actively involving two developers in the development process, pair programming ensures that the code is comprehensively reviewed, leading to a higher quality end product.

Additionally, pair programming plays a vital role in managing project risks and dependencies. Collaboration between developers promotes shared understanding and helps in mitigating potential roadblocks. By providing instant feedback and ensuring constant communication, the practice ensures that the project stays on track, adheres to the Agile values of adaptability and flexibility, and meets the desired project goals and objectives.

Pair Testing

Pair testing is a collaborative testing technique commonly used in the context of Agile Process and Project Management disciplines. It involves two individuals working together to test a software or system in an interactive manner. Each pair consists of a tester and an observer, where the tester performs the actual testing while the observer provides feedback, suggestions, and takes note of any issues identified.

The main objective of pair testing is to leverage the different perspectives, knowledge, and skills of the individuals involved to enhance the quality of the testing process and the overall product. By working together, the pair can identify more defects, generate better test scenarios, and improve the overall effectiveness of the testing efforts.

In an Agile environment, where quick iterations and continuous integration are essential, pair testing can be particularly beneficial. It promotes communication, knowledge sharing, and collaboration among team members, allowing for faster identification and resolution of issues. Additionally, pair testing helps to distribute testing knowledge within the team, reducing dependencies and enabling other team members to step in if needed.

Furthermore, pair testing is a valuable tool in project management disciplines as it ensures that testing activities are not solely reliant on a single individual. By involving multiple team members in the testing process, it mitigates the risk of bottlenecks and brings different perspectives to the table, resulting in a more comprehensive and rigorous testing approach.

Pair Writing

The Agile Process is a project management approach that emphasizes flexibility, collaboration, and iterative development. It is based on the principles outlined in the Agile Manifesto, which include valuing individuals and interactions, working software, customer collaboration, and responding to change.

Agile Project Management is a discipline that involves planning, organizing, and managing projects using Agile processes. It focuses on delivering value to customers in shorter timeframes by breaking the project into smaller, manageable tasks, and continuously adapting and adjusting the plans as needed.

Paper Prototyping Kits

A paper prototyping kit is a physical toolkit that is used in the context of Design Thinking disciplines to create low-fidelity prototypes of digital or physical products. It provides a collection of tools and materials that enable designers to quickly and easily sketch, cut, and assemble various elements that communicate the basic functionality and layout of a product.

The purpose of a paper prototyping kit is to facilitate the iterative process of exploring and refining design ideas through quick and inexpensive mock-ups. It allows designers to rapidly test different concepts, iterate on the design, and gather valuable feedback from stakeholders or potential users before investing time and resources in building a high-fidelity prototype or a final product.

Paper Prototyping

Paper prototyping is a technique used in the field of design thinking to create a visual representation of a product or service using simple, hand-drawn sketches on paper. It is an essential tool in the early stages of the design process as it allows designers to quickly and iteratively explore and refine their ideas.

The process involves creating a series of screens or elements that represent the different components and interactions of the product or service. These screens are then arranged in a sequence that simulates the user experience. By physically manipulating the paper prototypes, designers can observe and evaluate the flow and usability of the design, identify any issues or improvements, and make necessary adjustments.

Personas

Personas, in the context of Agile Process and Project Management disciplines, are fictional representations of the target users or customers of a product or service. They are created based on research and analysis of the actual users or customers to help project teams better understand and relate to their needs, goals, behaviors, and preferences.

Personas serve as archetypal user profiles that capture the characteristics, motivations, and pain points of different user segments. They enable project teams to design and deliver products or services that align with the target users' requirements and expectations. Personas also help in making informed decisions throughout the development lifecycle, guiding the team in prioritizing features, making design choices, and evaluating the effectiveness of the product or service.

Pig And Chicken

Pig and Chicken are two terms often used in the context of Agile Process and Project Management disciplines.

In Agile, the concept of the Pig and Chicken metaphor is used to distinguish the level of commitment and involvement of team members in a project. The metaphor originates from the story of a chicken and a pig discussing the idea of opening a restaurant, with the chicken suggesting they serve bacon and eggs. The chicken is involved but the pig is committed, as it would have to contribute its own flesh.

Similarly, in an Agile project, the Pig represents the team members who are fully committed and directly involved in the project's delivery. They are the individuals responsible for executing tasks, making decisions, and delivering the work. These team members have a significant stake in the project's success. Their commitment is measured by their sustained involvement and accountability throughout the project's duration.

On the other hand, the Chicken refers to individuals who are involved in the project but are not committed to the same extent as the Pigs. They may include stakeholders, observers, or managers who have an interest in the project's outcome. While their contribution and input are valuable, they do not have the same level of accountability as the Pigs.

The Pig and Chicken metaphor helps to emphasize the importance of commitment and accountability in Agile projects. It encourages active involvement and ownership from the team members who are dedicated to delivering value and meeting project objectives. By recognizing and distinguishing the level of commitment, Agile teams can ensure effective collaboration and shared responsibility, leading to a higher likelihood of project success.

Pipeline

A pipeline in the context of Agile Process and Project Management disciplines refers to a set of interconnected stages or phases that a project or task goes through from initiation to completion. It represents the flow and progression of work within a team or organization, ensuring a systematic and structured approach to project execution.

In an Agile environment, a pipeline is typically composed of several stages, such as planning, development, testing, and deployment. Each stage represents a distinct set of activities and tasks that need to be completed before moving on to the next stage. The pipeline helps teams visualize and manage the progress of work, enabling them to track and monitor the status of each task or feature throughout its lifecycle.

The pipeline approach promotes transparency, collaboration, and continuous improvement. It allows for feedback loops and adjustments at each stage, ensuring that the project stays on track and meets the changing requirements and expectations of stakeholders. By breaking down the work into smaller, manageable chunks, the pipeline enables teams to focus on delivering value incrementally, making it easier to adapt to evolving customer needs and market conditions.

Moreover, the pipeline facilitates efficient resource allocation and optimization. It helps in identifying bottlenecks, dependencies, and potential risks early on, allowing teams to take proactive measures and make informed decisions to mitigate them. With a clear understanding of the pipeline, team members can prioritize tasks, allocate resources effectively, and improve overall productivity and efficiency in project execution.

Planning Poker

Planning Poker is a collaborative estimation technique used in Agile Process and Project Management disciplines to determine the effort or complexity required to complete specific tasks or user stories. It is a variation of the Wideband Delphi method, specifically tailored for Agile teams.

During a Planning Poker session, a group of team members, typically including the Product Owner, Scrum Master, and development team, come together to estimate the relative size of backlog items. The items can vary from user stories, features, bug fixes, or any other work items identified for the project.

The process begins with a facilitator presenting a backlog item to the team. Each team member then selects a card from a deck of Planning Poker cards. These cards have numerical values representing the effort or complexity of the task, such as the Fibonacci sequence (1, 2, 3, 5, 8, 13, etc.) or the T-Shirt sizes (XS, S, M, L, XL, etc.).

Once everyone has chosen a card, the facilitator asks each team member to reveal their card simultaneously. In case of significant differences in estimation, the team members who chose the highest and lowest values discuss their reasoning for their estimation. This helps uncover and address any misunderstandings or knowledge gaps within the team.

After the discussion, the team members independently select cards again until a consensus is reached. The consensus is typically achieved when all team members reveal the same card value, indicating agreement on the effort required for the backlog item.

Planning Poker promotes collaboration, transparency, and engagement within the Agile team, leading to more accurate estimations and better alignment on project goals. It helps in prioritizing work and providing stakeholders with a better understanding of the team's capacity and expected delivery timelines.

Principled Innovation

Principled Innovation refers to the application of ethical principles and values in the practice of Design Thinking disciplines. It involves considering the social, environmental, and economic impacts of innovations and ensuring that the solutions developed are not only technically feasible and economically viable but also socially responsible.

In principled innovation, designers and innovators are guided by a set of principles such as inclusivity, transparency, and sustainability. They strive to create solutions that address the needs and aspirations of diverse stakeholders, leaving no one behind. They also prioritize transparency by involving stakeholders in the design process and making the decision-making procedures clear and accountable.

Furthermore, principled innovation considers the long-term impacts of design solutions on the environment. It seeks to develop sustainable solutions that minimize resource consumption, reduce waste, and promote ecological balance. This involves incorporating circular economy principles, such as designing for reusability and recyclability, into the innovation process.

In summary, principled innovation in Design Thinking disciplines involves applying ethical principles and values, considering social, environmental, and economic impacts, and creating solutions that are inclusive, transparent, and sustainable. It aims to ensure that innovations not only meet the immediate needs of users but also contribute to a better and more equitable future for society and the planet.

Prioritization

Prioritization in the context of Agile Process and Project Management disciplines refers to the act of arranging or organizing tasks, features, or requirements based on their relative importance or value.

In Agile methodologies, such as Scrum or Kanban, prioritization plays a crucial role in managing and delivering projects effectively. It involves categorizing the features or user stories in a product backlog or task list based on their priority. The priority is typically determined by the product owner or project stakeholders, taking into consideration various factors such as customer needs, business objectives, market demands, and technical dependencies.

Problem Exploration

Problem Exploration is a crucial phase in the Design Thinking disciplines that involves gaining a deep understanding of the problem at hand. It entails thorough research and analysis to identify the root causes, uncover hidden insights, and define the problem statement accurately.

During the Problem Exploration phase, the design team immerses themselves in the context of the problem, taking a holistic approach to understand the various perspectives and factors involved. This may include conducting interviews, surveys, observations, and gathering relevant data to gain valuable insights into the user's needs, desires, and challenges.

The goal of Problem Exploration is to uncover the underlying needs and motivations of the users and stakeholders. By empathizing with their experience, the design team can identify pain points, gaps, and opportunities for innovation. This phase also helps in reframing the problem statement, ensuring that it aligns with the user's perspective and addresses their core needs.

A successful Problem Exploration requires a curious and open mindset, allowing the design team to challenge assumptions, explore different angles, and gather diverse perspectives. It involves synthesizing the collected information to generate meaningful insights and formulating a clear problem statement that guides the subsequent phases of the Design Thinking process.

Problem Finding

Problem finding, in the context of Design Thinking disciplines, refers to the process of identifying and defining the core issues or challenges that need to be addressed in a design project. It involves understanding the user's needs, motivations, and pain points, as well as analyzing the current state of the problem or opportunity at hand.

The purpose of problem finding is to gain a deep understanding of the underlying problem, rather than jumping to solution mode prematurely. By thoroughly exploring and defining the problem, designers are able to generate more relevant and effective solutions that truly address the needs of the user.

Problem Framing Frameworks

A problem framing framework is a structured approach or tool used in the context of design thinking disciplines to define and understand the problem that needs to be solved. It provides a systematic way to analyze and clarify the problem, ensuring that the focus remains on the user's needs and desires. This framework helps to uncover underlying issues, uncover assumptions, and identify constraints or potential opportunities that may influence the problem definition and solution.

The goal of a problem framing framework is to create a shared understanding among the team members and stakeholders of the problem at hand. It helps to establish a clear problem statement and scope for the design challenge. By using this framework, designers can ensure that the problem is not overly narrow or broad, and that it aligns with the larger goals and objectives of the project.

Problem Framing Workshops

A problem framing workshop is a collaborative and iterative process used in the context of design thinking disciplines to define and refine the problem statement or challenge that needs to be addressed. It brings together multidisciplinary teams to identify the root cause of the problem, explore different perspectives, and synthesize insights to converge on a clear and actionable problem statement.

The workshop typically begins with a clear understanding of the problem space and the desired outcomes. Facilitators guide participants through structured activities such as brainstorming, mind mapping, and affinity diagrams to explore the dimensions of the problem and uncover its underlying complexities. The emphasis is on divergent thinking, encouraging participants to generate a wide range of ideas and perspectives without evaluation or judgment.

As the workshop progresses, participants analyze and refine their insights, identify patterns, and organize them into themes or categories. This helps in identifying key stakeholders, understanding their needs and expectations, and considering the broader context in which the problem exists. Collaborative activities such as empathy mapping and user journey mapping enable participants to develop a deeper understanding of the problem by empathizing with the experiences and needs of the end-users or stakeholders.

By the end of the problem framing workshop, participants converge on a well-defined problem statement that captures the essence of the challenge and provides a clear direction for subsequent ideation and solution development. The problem statement serves as a guiding light for the design process and helps in aligning the team's efforts towards a common goal. It also helps in avoiding solution bias by ensuring that the problem is thoroughly understood before jumping into solutioning.

Problem Framing

Problem framing is the process of defining and articulating a specific problem to be solved within the context of design thinking disciplines. It involves developing a clear understanding of the problem by gathering relevant information and insights, identifying the root causes, and defining the scope and boundaries of the problem.

In design thinking, problem framing is a crucial step that sets the foundation for the entire design process. It helps designers and innovators to identify and interpret the needs and goals of the users or stakeholders, and to create meaningful solutions that address these needs effectively.

Problem Redefinition Kits

A Problem Redefinition Kit is a tool used in the context of Design Thinking disciplines to facilitate the process of problem definition and redefinition. It consists of a set of materials, prompts, and activities that guide individuals or teams through a structured and collaborative process of reframing and reframing the problem at hand.

The purpose of a Problem Redefinition Kit is to help individuals or teams gain a deeper understanding of the problem they are trying to solve and to generate innovative solutions. It encourages a shift in mindset by challenging preconceived notions and assumptions about the problem, and by promoting a more empathetic and user-centered approach.

Problem Redefinition Techniques

Problem redefinition is a technique employed in the field of design thinking to approach problem-solving from a different perspective. It involves stepping back from the initial problem statement and challenging its assumptions, constraints, and framing in order to uncover new insights and opportunities for innovation.

This technique recognizes that problems are often defined too narrowly or based on incomplete information, which can limit the potential solutions. By redefining the problem, designers aim to gain a deeper and more comprehensive understanding of the issue at hand, enabling them to generate more creative and effective solutions.

Problem Redefinition

Problem Redefinition is a crucial step in the Design Thinking process that involves reframing the initial problem statement into a more meaningful and insightful challenge, leading to innovative and effective solutions. It aims to broaden the perspective and deepen the understanding of the problem by exploring different angles, contexts, and stakeholders involved.

This process begins by critically examining the initial problem statement and questioning its assumptions, constraints, and potential biases. It encourages designers to step back and challenge the status quo, fostering a mindset of curiosity and openness to new possibilities. By doing so, it helps to uncover underlying needs, motivations, and root causes that may have been overlooked initially.

Problem Reframing

The problem reframing is a key concept in the Design Thinking disciplines, which involves shifting the perspective and redefining the problem statement in order to discover innovative solutions. It requires approaching the problem from different angles and exploring alternative interpretations and viewpoints.

The process of problem reframing entails challenging the initial assumptions and preconceived notions about the problem. It involves investigating the underlying causes and root issues that contribute to the problem, rather than focusing solely on the symptoms. By reframing the problem, designers can gain a deeper understanding of the context, user needs, and constraints, which is crucial for generating creative and effective solutions.

Problem Solving

Problem solving in the context of Design Thinking disciplines refers to the process of identifying, understanding, and resolving complex problems through a user-centric approach. It involves a systematic and collaborative approach that focuses on finding innovative and effective solutions to address user needs and challenges.

The problem-solving process in Design Thinking typically follows several stages, including empathizing, defining, ideating, prototyping, and testing. These stages encourage a deep understanding of the problem by empathizing with the user, defining the problem statement, generating a wide range of ideas, creating prototypes to visualize concepts, and testing these prototypes to gather feedback for iteration.

Problem Space

Problem Space is a term used in Design Thinking disciplines to refer to the context or environment in which a problem exists. It encompasses the various factors, constraints, and complexities that influence the problem and need to be considered during the design process.

A problem space can be seen as a holistic view of the problem, taking into account not only the immediate issue at hand but also the broader system in which it is embedded. This includes understanding the needs and perspectives of various stakeholders, identifying any underlying dependencies or interconnections, and considering the potential impact of the solution on different aspects of the problem space.

Problem-Based Learning

Problem-Based Learning (PBL) is a pedagogical approach within Design Thinking disciplines that emphasizes active, student-centered learning by presenting students with real-world problems or challenges to solve. It is a learner-centered approach that promotes critical thinking, collaboration, and problem-solving skills.

In PBL, students are tasked with identifying and analyzing complex problems, conducting independent research, and developing viable solutions. They work in small teams or individually to explore the problem space, gather relevant information, and propose innovative solutions. This process encourages students to apply their existing knowledge and skills while also acquiring new ones through the challenges they face.

Process Enhancement

Process Enhancement is a Design Thinking discipline that focuses on improving and optimizing existing processes within an organization. It involves critically analyzing the current workflow, identifying inefficiencies or bottlenecks, and implementing strategic changes to enhance overall productivity and effectiveness.

The Process Enhancement approach follows a structured methodology that includes several key steps. Firstly, it involves understanding the problem or pain points associated with the existing process through research and data analysis. This step helps to gather insights and identify the specific areas that require improvement.

Once the problem areas are identified, the next step is to ideate and brainstorm potential solutions. This is done by involving stakeholders and cross-functional teams to collectively generate innovative ideas that can address the identified challenges.

After ideation, the focus shifts towards prototyping and testing the proposed solutions. This step involves creating small-scale prototypes or mock-ups of the new processes and conducting pilot tests to evaluate their feasibility and effectiveness. Feedback and insights gained from the testing phase are then used to refine and iterate the prototypes, ensuring that the final solution is optimized for implementation.

Finally, the last step in Process Enhancement is the implementation stage. This involves executing the refined solution, monitoring its performance, and making any necessary adjustments to ensure continuous improvement. It is crucial to involve all relevant stakeholders and provide adequate training and support during the implementation phase to ensure successful adoption and integration of the enhanced process.

Process Improvement

Process improvement refers to the systematic approach of identifying, analyzing, and enhancing existing processes to optimize efficiency, effectiveness, and overall performance. It is a critical aspect of Design Thinking disciplines as it enables continuous learning and innovation.

Through process improvement, organizations are able to identify and eliminate bottlenecks, unnecessary steps, and inefficiencies in their processes. By doing so, they can streamline operations, reduce costs, improve quality, and enhance customer satisfaction. It involves gathering data, analyzing it to identify areas of improvement, brainstorming potential solutions, implementing changes, and measuring the impact of those changes.

Process Innovation

Process innovation, within the context of Design Thinking disciplines, refers to the creation and implementation of novel methods and approaches to enhance the efficiency, effectiveness, and value of a specific process or set of processes. It involves reimagining and transforming existing processes, systems, and practices, aiming to generate new and improved ways of accomplishing tasks, delivering products or services, and addressing challenges.

Process innovation is driven by a deep understanding of the users' needs and experiences, as well as a holistic and empathetic perspective. It leverages design thinking principles to identify pain points, uncover opportunities, and generate innovative solutions that can optimize workflows, eliminate inefficiencies, and enhance overall performance. By adopting a human-centered approach, process innovation seeks to align the organization's goals with the desires and expectations of the end-users.

Process Mapping

Process mapping is a crucial step in the Design Thinking disciplines that involves visually representing and analyzing the flow and sequence of activities, decisions, and information within a process. It helps teams gain a clear understanding of how a process currently operates and identifies areas for improvement and optimization.

By creating a visual representation, designers and teams can identify bottlenecks, redundancies, and inefficiencies within the process. This enables them to eliminate unnecessary steps, streamline workflows, and introduce innovative solutions. Process mapping provides a comprehensive view of the entire process, capturing both the big picture and the minute details.

Process Refinement

Process refinement is a key component of the Design Thinking discipline, which involves continuously improving and optimizing the various stages and activities of the design process.

It is a structured approach that focuses on enhancing the efficiency, effectiveness, and overall quality of the design process, with the ultimate goal of delivering better outcomes for users, customers, and stakeholders.

Process Visualization

Process Visualization is a key aspect of Design Thinking that involves creating visual representations to communicate and understand complex processes. It is a strategic tool that allows designers and stakeholders to gain insights, analyze, and optimize processes by making them more transparent and accessible.

Through Process Visualization, designers can break down complicated concepts into simple and intuitive visuals, such as diagrams, flowcharts, or interactive prototypes. These visual representations help to communicate ideas and thoughts effectively, enabling collaboration among team members and stakeholders who may have different levels of understanding or expertise.

Product Backlog

The product backlog is a prioritized list of all desired functionalities, enhancements, and bug fixes for a product. It is a living document that evolves throughout the project, and serves as a central repository of requirements for the development team. In the Agile process, the product backlog is maintained by the product owner, who is responsible for gathering user requirements, managing stakeholder expectations, and ensuring that the backlog is aligned with the overall project vision. The product owner collaborates closely with the development team to refine and prioritize backlog items. Each item in the product backlog is described in sufficient detail to provide understanding to the development team. The level of detail required may vary depending on the team's preference, but it should always convey the intended value or outcome of the item. The backlog items are typically written in a user story format, using the following template: "As a [role], I want [goal] so that [benefit]." The product backlog is regularly reviewed and reprioritized during backlog refinement sessions and sprint planning meetings. The development team collectively estimates the effort required to implement each item, enabling the product owner to make informed decisions about prioritization. Throughout the project, the product backlog serves as a communication tool, facilitating transparency and alignment between the product owner, development team, and other stakeholders. It allows the team to plan and prioritize work based on business value and customer needs, ensuring that the most valuable features are delivered first. Overall, the product backlog is a key artifact in Agile project management, enabling iterative and incremental development by providing a clear and prioritized list of requirements for the development team to work on.

Product Ecosystem

A product ecosystem refers to the interconnected network of products, services, and technologies that work together to fulfill a specific user need or solve a problem. It encompasses all the components, both physical and digital, that are required for the product to function and provide value to its users.

Design thinking disciplines involve considering the entire product ecosystem when creating and developing a new product. This approach emphasizes understanding the context in which the product will be used and the various interactions and relationships it will have with other products, services, and stakeholders. By taking a holistic view of the ecosystem, designers can identify opportunities for innovation, collaboration, and enhancement.

Product Increment

Product Increment is a term used in the Agile Process and Project Management disciplines to refer to the tangible outcome of a development sprint or iteration in an Agile project. It is a functional, usable piece of the product that adds value to the end-users or stakeholders. The Product Increment represents a small, complete portion of the overall product, which can be potentially released to the market or demonstrated to stakeholders.

In an Agile project, development work is divided into time-boxed iterations called sprints. At the end of each sprint, the development team delivers a working, shippable increment of the product. This increment is a result of the team's collaboration, feedback, and continuous improvement throughout the sprint. The Product Increment encompasses the completed user stories, features, enhancements, bug fixes, or any other deliverables that were planned and committed for the sprint.

The key characteristic of a Product Increment is that it should be usable and valuable on its own, even if it is not the full, final version of the product. This means that each increment should provide real functionality and benefits to the end-users or stakeholders. It allows the project team to receive early feedback, validate assumptions, and make necessary adjustments in subsequent sprints.

The Product Increment serves as a concrete representation of the progress made by the team, demonstrating their ability to deliver working product increments within short iterations. It also enables stakeholders to inspect and adapt the product early in the development process. This iterative and incremental approach ensures that the project stays on track, aligns with customer requirements, and delivers value throughout the project lifecycle.

Product Owner Team

A Product Owner Team is a group of individuals responsible for defining and prioritizing the features and requirements of a product in an Agile project. They work closely with stakeholders to ensure that the product meets the needs of the end users and aligns with the vision and goals of the organization.

In an Agile development process, the Product Owner Team plays a crucial role in gathering and refining the product backlog, which consists of a prioritized list of user stories and requirements. They work closely with the development team to clarify and provide necessary details for each item in the backlog, ensuring that the team has a clear understanding of what needs to be delivered.

The Product Owner Team regularly engages with stakeholders to gather feedback and incorporate it into the product backlog. They prioritize the backlog based on business value and customer needs, making sure that the most valuable and important features are delivered early on. As the development progresses, the team ensures that the backlog is updated and adjusted based on new information and changing requirements.

Throughout the project, the Product Owner Team acts as a bridge between the development team and stakeholders, ensuring that communication is clear and expectations are managed. They provide guidance and clarification to the development team, answering questions and seeking resolutions to any issues that arise during the development process.

Product Owner

A Product Owner is a key role in Agile Process and Project Management disciplines. Their primary responsibility is to understand the needs of the stakeholders and translate them into actionable product requirements. They work closely with the development team to ensure that the product vision is achieved.

The Product Owner is the voice of the customer or end user. They gather feedback, prioritize feature requests, and make decisions based on what will provide the most value to the customer. They are responsible for creating and maintaining the product backlog, which is a prioritized list of user stories or features that need to be developed. They also define and communicate the product vision and ensure that it aligns with the goals of the organization.

Product Roadmap

A product roadmap, in the context of Agile Process and Project Management disciplines, is a high-level strategic plan that outlines the vision and direction for a product or service. It serves as a dynamic communication tool that visually illustrates the goals, milestones, and key features of the product in a concise and easily digestible manner.

The product roadmap plays a crucial role in guiding the development team and stakeholders by providing a clear understanding of the product's overall trajectory. It helps align business objectives with user needs and market dynamics, facilitating collaboration and decision-making throughout the development lifecycle.

Product Vision

A product vision is a clear and concise description of the overall goals and objectives for a product. It serves as a guiding statement that outlines the desired future state of the product, including its purpose, target audience, and value proposition.

In the context of Agile Process and Project Management, the product vision plays a crucial role in providing a shared understanding of what the team is working towards. It acts as a compass, helping to align the efforts of all stakeholders and ensuring that everyone is moving in the same direction.

The product vision should be inspiring and motivating, capturing the essence of what the product is and why it matters. It should communicate the key benefits and value that the product will deliver to its users or customers.

In Agile development, the product vision is often communicated through a vision statement, which is a concise and memorable statement that captures the essence of the product. This statement should be easily understood and remembered by all team members, providing a constant reminder of the larger purpose and goals of the project.

Ultimately, the product vision serves as a North Star, providing clarity and focus throughout the development process. It helps to prioritize work, make informed decisions, and ensure that the final product meets the needs and expectations of its intended audience.

Productivity

Productivity in the context of Agile Process and Project Management disciplines refers to the effective and efficient use of resources, time, and effort to achieve the desired results and deliver value. It entails maximizing output while minimizing waste, optimizing workflow, and consistently meeting project goals and deadlines.

In Agile, productivity is measured not only by the quantity of work completed but also by the quality and value of the deliverables. It emphasizes adaptability, collaboration, and continuous improvement. Agile teams focus on delivering smaller increments of work, known as iterations or sprints, and frequently review and adjust their processes to enhance productivity.

Progressive Disclosure

Progressive disclosure is a design principle used in the context of Design Thinking disciplines, aimed at simplifying complex information and interactions for users. It involves gradually revealing information or functionality as the user engages with a system or interface, allowing for a more intuitive and manageable user experience.

This principle is particularly important in situations where overwhelming users with too much information or too many options can lead to confusion, frustration, and decision paralysis. By progressively disclosing information or functionality, designers can create a smoother learning curve and prevent cognitive overload.

Prototype Testing Labs

A prototype testing lab is a specialized facility or team within a design thinking discipline that focuses on evaluating and validating prototypes before they are implemented or brought to market. The primary aim of prototype testing is to gather feedback and insights from potential users or stakeholders to identify any flaws, areas of improvement, or potential opportunities for innovation.

Prototype testing labs employ a variety of methods and tools to conduct their evaluations. These may include user testing, where individuals interact with the prototype and provide feedback on its usability, functionality, and overall experience. Usability testing often involves observing and recording participants' behaviors, preferences, and pain points. Prototype testing may also involve gathering quantitative data through surveys, questionnaires, or analytics software, which can help measure user satisfaction, product performance, or the effectiveness of specific design features.

Prototype Testing

Prototype testing is a crucial stage in the design thinking process where a preliminary version of a product or service is evaluated and validated. It involves testing and gathering feedback on the prototype's functionality, usability, and desirability to identify areas of improvement and refine the concept.

During prototype testing, users or potential customers interact with the prototype, allowing designers and stakeholders to gain valuable insights into the user experience. The testing phase facilitates a deeper understanding of users' needs, preferences, and pain points, which can inform further design decisions.

Psychological Safety

Psychological safety refers to an individual's perception of the work environment, where they feel safe to take risks, express their opinions, and be vulnerable without fearing negative consequences. Within the Agile Process and Project Management disciplines, psychological safety plays a crucial role in promoting collaboration, innovation, and effective team dynamics.

Agile methodologies value self-organizing teams that are empowered to make decisions, share knowledge, and provide feedback. Psychological safety within these environments allows team members to feel comfortable contributing their ideas, asking questions, and challenging assumptions. This willingness to speak up and share valuable insights fosters a culture of trust and open communication, enabling teams to adapt and learn from both successes and failures.

In Agile Project Management, psychological safety is particularly important as it encourages team members to experiment, take on new challenges, and suggest process improvements. When individuals feel psychologically safe, they are more inclined to learn from mistakes and take risks, ultimately leading to continuous improvement and innovation within the project.

Overall, psychological safety in Agile embraces diversity of thought, encourages healthy conflict, and provides an environment where individuals are not afraid to express their thoughts and concerns. It enables teams to capitalize on the collective intelligence and creativity of its members, facilitating higher levels of performance, commitment, and satisfaction.

Pull System

A pull system is a concept used in Agile Process and Project Management disciplines to manage and control the flow of work in a project. It is a methodology that focuses on optimizing the efficiency and effectiveness of a project by allowing work to be pulled as needed, rather than pushing work onto team members.

In a pull system, work is not assigned or pushed to individuals or teams. Instead, team members are empowered to pull work from a common backlog based on their capacity and expertise. This approach promotes self-organization and encourages individuals to take ownership of their work.

Pull-Based System

A pull-based system is a key concept in Agile Process and Project Management disciplines, referring to a method of work allocation and task prioritization that allows team members to self-organize and pull work based on their own capacity and expertise.

In a pull-based system, work is not assigned or pushed onto individuals or teams by a central authority, but rather made available for them to pull or take on at their discretion. This approach promotes flexibility, collaboration, and individual accountability, and is often seen as a fundamental principle of Agile methodologies.

Quality Assurance

Quality Assurance in the context of Agile Process and Project Management disciplines refers to the systematic and proactive approach taken to ensure that the software development process and the resulting product adhere to the required standards and specifications. It involves ongoing monitoring and evaluation of the entire development lifecycle to identify any deviations or deficiencies and take corrective actions as necessary.

In Agile, Quality Assurance is integrated throughout the development process rather than being a separate phase at the end. It is an integral part of the iterative and incremental nature of Agile methodologies, where continuous feedback and improvement are emphasized. Quality Assurance activities are carried out by a dedicated team or individuals who work closely with the development team and stakeholders to ensure that quality is maintained at every stage.

RAD (Rapid Application Development)

Rapid Application Development (RAD) is an iterative software development approach that emphasizes quick prototyping and continuous user feedback.

In the context of Agile Process and Project Management disciplines, RAD is based on the principles of agility, collaboration, and iterative development. It focuses on delivering software applications in short iterations, enabling frequent releases and continuous user engagement.

RAD is characterized by its four key principles:

1. Active User Involvement: RAD promotes active involvement of end-users throughout the development process. Users provide feedback on the prototypes and can influence the direction of the application, ensuring it aligns with their needs and expectations.

2. Rapid Iterations: RAD involves breaking down the project into multiple shorter iterations, typically lasting a few weeks. Each iteration focuses on developing a specific portion of the application. The emphasis on speed helps in faster delivery and reduces the risk of developing features that may no longer be relevant.

3. Prototyping: RAD emphasizes the creation of quick and functional prototypes to gather user feedback. Prototypes capture the essential functionality of the application and are iteratively refined based on user input. This approach enables developers to make adjustments and enhancements on-the-fly, ensuring the final product caters to user needs.

4. Timeboxing: RAD relies on strict timeboxing to manage project timelines and ensure timely delivery. Each iteration is timeboxed, allowing developers to set achievable goals and maintain a focus on meeting deadlines.

RAD offers several benefits when applied in Agile Process and Project Management disciplines. It fosters collaboration between developers, users, and stakeholders, resulting in a better understanding of requirements and increased project success. By involving end-users in the process, RAD reduces the risk of building software that does not meet their needs. Additionally, the iterative nature of RAD allows for flexibility and adaptation to changing requirements, enhancing overall project agility.

Rapid Feedback

Rapid feedback refers to the process of continuously and quickly eliciting, collecting, and incorporating input, opinions, and observations from stakeholders in order to inform and improve the progress, quality, and outcomes of a project or initiative.

In the context of Agile Process and Project Management disciplines, rapid feedback is a fundamental principle and practice that enables teams and organizations to be responsive, adaptable, and customer-centric. It emphasizes the importance of iterative cycles of communication and interaction with stakeholders, including customers, users, team members, and management.

Rapid Testing

Rapid Testing in the context of Design Thinking disciplines refers to the efficient and iterative process of testing design hypotheses and prototypes to gather feedback and validate assumptions. It is a key component of the design thinking methodology, as it allows designers and teams to quickly and iteratively identify and address potential issues and improvements in their designs.

The goal of rapid testing is to minimize the time and cost required to validate design concepts and obtain user feedback. By testing early and often, designers can gain a deeper understanding of user needs and preferences and make informed design decisions based on real user feedback. This approach helps to minimize the risk of developing a product or service that fails to meet user expectations.

Rapid Validation Kits

Rapid Validation Kits are tools used in the Design Thinking process to quickly and efficiently test and validate ideas, concepts, or prototypes. These kits are designed to facilitate the rapid collection of meaningful feedback and insights from users or stakeholders, enabling the team to make informed decisions and iterate on their designs.

The purpose of a Rapid Validation Kit is to provide a structured and systematic approach to the validation phase of the Design Thinking process. The kit typically consists of a set of materials, guidelines, and templates that guide the team through the validation process, helping them to define clear objectives, identify relevant hypotheses, and design effective experiments.

The key components of a Rapid Validation Kit may include interview scripts, survey templates, usability testing protocols, and data collection methods. These tools are specifically tailored to the needs of the validation phase, allowing the team to efficiently gather feedback from users and stakeholders, analyze the data, and derive insights to inform further iterations.

By using a Rapid Validation Kit, teams can save time and resources by quickly identifying which ideas or concepts are viable and have the potential for success. The structured nature of the kit ensures that the team follows a consistent and replicable process for validation, reducing bias and increasing the reliability of the results.

Overall, Rapid Validation Kits are essential tools for design teams looking to validate their ideas and prototypes quickly and effectively. They provide a framework and set of tools that enable teams to collect valuable feedback, refine their designs, and make data-driven decisions in the design process.

Rapid Validation Platforms

Rapid validation platforms are tools or systems used in the context of Design Thinking disciplines to rapidly test, validate, and iterate on ideas, concepts, or prototypes. These platforms enable fast and efficient feedback and validation from users, stakeholders, or target audiences, helping designers to make informed decisions and refine their designs.

These platforms typically provide various methods or techniques for gathering feedback and insights, such as surveys, interviews, usability testing, A/B testing, or user analytics. They may also offer features for creating interactive prototypes, conducting remote usability sessions, or collecting data for quantitative analysis.

Rapid Validation

Rapid Validation is a process used in the context of Design Thinking disciplines to quickly and efficiently validate ideas, assumptions, and potential solutions.

In the design thinking process, rapid validation involves selecting a specific idea or solution and testing it on a small scale to determine its viability and potential impact. This process is crucial in the early stages of design thinking, as it allows designers to gather feedback and make informed decisions on whether to continue developing an idea or pivot to a different approach.

Refactoring

Refactoring is a disciplined technique used in Agile Process and Project Management disciplines to improve the design and structure of existing code without changing its external behavior.

Refactoring involves making small, incremental changes to the codebase to enhance its maintainability, readability, and extensibility. It is a continuous process that aims to remove code smells, eliminate duplication, and simplify complex logic, thereby improving the overall quality of the code.

Refinement

Agile Process:

The Agile Process is a project management approach that emphasizes flexibility and adaptability in the development and execution of tasks and deliverables. It involves breaking down larger projects into smaller, more manageable iterations called "sprints." These sprints typically last between one to four weeks, during which a set of specific tasks are completed and reviewed.

Agile Project Management:

Agile Project Management is a framework for managing and overseeing projects within the Agile Process. It involves the use of iterative and incremental methods to deliver high-quality results in a timely manner. The primary role of an Agile Project Manager is to facilitate communication and collaboration among team members while ensuring that project goals are met.

Reflection

Reflection is a crucial step in the Design Thinking process that involves analyzing and evaluating the outcomes and experiences gained throughout the various disciplines of Design Thinking. It provides a structured framework to examine the successes, failures, and learnings from each stage of the process, allowing for continuous improvement and innovation.

Through reflection, designers are able to gain insights into their own thinking, biases, and assumptions, as well as gather feedback from users and stakeholders. This self-reflection helps them identify areas for improvement and discover new opportunities for creative problem-solving.

Reframe The Problem

The problem reframing in the context of Design Thinking disciplines refers to the act of reassessing and redefining the problem statement in a way that allows for innovative and creative solutions to be generated. It involves shifting the focus from the initial problem statement to uncover the underlying needs, motivations, and perspectives of the users or stakeholders.

By reframing the problem, Design Thinkers challenge assumptions and break free from traditional problem-solving paradigms. They aim to gain a deeper understanding of the problem's root causes, explore different perspectives, and identify new opportunities for solving it. This process often involves empathizing with the end-users, conducting research, generating insights, and iterating on potential solutions.

Remote Collaboration Software

Remote Collaboration Software refers to digital tools or platforms that enable individuals or teams to work together, regardless of their physical location, in a seamless and efficient manner. It facilitates communication, collaboration, and innovation among geographically dispersed members involved in Design Thinking disciplines.

Design Thinking is a problem-solving approach that places emphasis on understanding users' needs, generating diverse ideas, prototyping, and continuously iterating to create effective solutions. It promotes a human-centered design approach by fostering empathy, collaboration, and experimentation.

In the context of Design Thinking, Remote Collaboration Software provides a virtual environment where designers, researchers, stakeholders, and other team members can collaborate in real time. It offers features such as video conferencing, screen sharing, file sharing, and collaborative whiteboards. These tools eliminate the need for physical proximity and enable multidisciplinary teams to work together efficiently, leveraging their collective creativity and expertise.

The software enhances the collaboration process by allowing team members to engage in productive discussions, share ideas, co-create, and gather feedback remotely. It supports the visualization of concepts through digital sketching and prototyping. Furthermore, it facilitates the sharing and review of design artifacts, user research findings, and other relevant documents.

Remote Collaboration Software also provides a central repository for project-related information and documentation, ensuring that all team members have access to the latest updates and can contribute effectively. It promotes transparency and accountability among team members by enabling them to track and monitor progress, assign tasks, and share project timelines.

In conclusion, Remote Collaboration Software is a valuable tool in Design Thinking disciplines as it enables geographically dispersed teams to effectively collaborate, communicate, and innovate, fostering a more inclusive and human-centered design process.

Remote Usability Labs

Remote Usability Labs refer to a method in Design Thinking disciplines that involve conducting user research and testing remotely. In traditional usability labs, participants are observed while interacting with a product or prototype in a controlled environment. This approach allows designers and researchers to gain insights into user behavior, preferences, and pain points.

However, remote usability labs offer the advantage of conducting the same observations and testing activities remotely, without the need for physical presence. This method utilizes various tools and technologies to facilitate remote research and testing, such as video conferencing, screen sharing, and remote access to the prototype. Remote usability labs allow designers and researchers to overcome geographical barriers and engage with participants from different locations.

Remote Usability Testing Labs

Remote usability testing labs are facilities that are specifically designed to facilitate user testing and evaluation of digital products, services, or platforms. These labs provide a controlled environment for researchers and designers to observe and analyze user behavior, attitudes, and interactions with a digital interface, even when participants are located remotely.

Remote usability testing labs typically consist of a camera-equipped room or space where participants can interact with a digital product or interface, while their actions and facial expressions are recorded. These labs are equipped with technology that allows for remote monitoring and recording of participant sessions, ensuring that researchers and designers can observe and document user behavior in real-time.

One of the key advantages of remote usability testing labs is that they eliminate geographical barriers, allowing researchers to conduct studies with participants located anywhere in the world. This is particularly valuable in Design Thinking disciplines, where gaining insights from a diverse range of users is crucial for identifying and addressing usability challenges and improving the overall user experience.

Furthermore, remote usability testing labs provide researchers and designers with the flexibility to schedule and conduct user testing sessions at their convenience. Through the use of screen-sharing and videoconferencing technologies, participants can engage in the testing process from the comfort of their own location, maximizing convenience and minimizing logistical challenges.

Responsiveness

Responsiveness in the context of Agile Process and Project Management disciplines refers to the ability to quickly and effectively respond to changes and feedback throughout the project lifecycle. It is a fundamental principle of Agile methodologies, which prioritize adaptability and collaboration over rigid planning and documentation.

In Agile, responsiveness is achieved through iterative and incremental development, where project requirements and solutions evolve through the collaborative efforts of self-organizing and cross-functional teams. The Agile approach recognizes the inherent uncertainty and complexity of many projects, and embraces the need for regular feedback and adjustments to ensure the project's success.

Retrospective

A retrospective, in the context of Agile Process and Project Management disciplines, is a meeting that occurs at the end of a project iteration or sprint. Its purpose is to reflect on the project's progress, identify areas for improvement, and make adjustments for future iterations.

During a retrospective, the project team, including the Scrum Master, product owner, and development team, come together to review what went well, what didn't go well, and what can be done differently in the future. The meeting follows a structured format that allows for open and honest communication, ensuring that everyone's perspective is heard and considered.

The retrospective typically consists of three main phases: setting the stage, gathering data, and generating insights. In the "setting the stage" phase, the facilitator creates a safe space for the team to discuss and reflects on their experiences. This helps to establish an open and collaborative atmosphere for the meeting.

In the "gathering data" phase, the team identifies and collects relevant information about the project, such as the team's progress, challenges faced, and successes achieved. This information is gathered through various methods, such as group discussions, individual reflections, or anonymous surveys.

In the final phase, "generating insights," the team analyzes the data collected and identifies patterns or trends. They brainstorm potential improvements and create concrete action items that can be implemented in the next iteration or sprint. The goal here is to continuously improve the project's processes and outcomes.

Risk Burndown Chart

A Risk Burndown Chart is a visual representation of the progress made in mitigating or eliminating risks throughout a project's lifecycle in Agile Process and Project Management disciplines. It helps project teams and stakeholders to track and monitor the effectiveness of risk management strategies and identify areas that require more attention or improvement.

The chart typically consists of two axes. The horizontal axis represents the project timeline, divided into iterations or sprints. The vertical axis represents the level of risk, categorized into high, medium, and low. The chart starts with all identified risks represented at their initial levels on the vertical axis and progressively decreases as risks are mitigated or eliminated over time.

At the beginning of the project, the chart provides a snapshot of all identified risks and their severity, allowing the project team to prioritize and allocate resources accordingly. As the project progresses, risks are addressed through various risk management strategies, such as risk avoidance, risk transfer, risk mitigation, or risk acceptance. The chart is updated regularly to reflect the current status of each risk, allowing stakeholders to gauge the overall progress of risk management efforts.

By visually representing the reduction of risks over time, the Risk Burndown Chart enables project teams to identify trends, such as spikes in risk levels, and take proactive measures to prevent potential setbacks. It also provides transparency and enhances communication among team members and stakeholders, fostering a shared understanding of the project's risk landscape and promoting collaborative decision-making.

Risk Management

Risk management in the context of Agile Process and Project Management disciplines refers to the systematic process that identifies, analyzes, and mitigates potential risks that could impact the success of a project. It is a proactive approach that enables project teams to anticipate and address risks before they become major issues.

The Agile approach to risk management involves continuous monitoring and adaptation throughout the project lifecycle, as opposed to a one-time assessment at the beginning. This is because Agile projects are often characterized by changing requirements, dynamic environments, and evolving stakeholder expectations.

Scalability

Scalability, within the context of Agile Process and Project Management disciplines, refers to the ability of a system or process to handle increased workload or expansion without experiencing a decline in performance or efficiency. It denotes the system's capability to adapt and accommodate higher demands or increased complexity while maintaining its overall effectiveness.

In Agile Project Management, scalability plays a crucial role in ensuring the success and sustainability of projects. It involves designing and implementing a scalable framework that can effectively handle changes, growth, and evolving requirements throughout the project's lifecycle. This scalability allows teams to work collaboratively, react quickly to changes, and adapt their processes to meet new demands.

Scaled Agile Framework (SAFe)

The Scaled Agile Framework (SAFe) is a set of organizational and process guidelines that allow businesses to scale Agile practices across multiple teams, departments, or even entire organizations. It provides a structured approach to implement Agile principles in large-scale projects, ensuring alignment, collaboration, and efficient delivery.

SAFe builds upon the Agile Manifesto and encompasses Lean and systems thinking concepts to address the complexity and challenges faced by enterprises undertaking large-scale development initiatives. It consists of three primary levels: Team, Program, and Portfolio. At the Team level, SAFe emphasizes Agile principles like delivering value incrementally, ensuring continuous integration and deployment, and promoting self-organizing and cross-functional teams.

The Program level focuses on coordination and synchronization across multiple Agile teams working together to deliver a cohesive product or solution. SAFe provides guidance on practices such as Agile release trains, agile architecture, and system demos to facilitate collaboration, reduce dependencies, and improve overall system performance.

The Portfolio level, on the other hand, addresses strategic and investment decisions within the organization. It aims to align the organization's vision, goals, and business outcomes with Agile principles. SAFe provides tools and practices for strategic themes, portfolio epics, and governance to enable effective prioritization, resource allocation, and decision-making.

Overall, SAFe enables enterprises to scale Agile principles and practices while maintaining consistency, synchronization, and alignment across teams, projects, and organizational levels. It provides a framework that incorporates Agile principles into the larger enterprise context, offering a practical approach to achieve successful Agile transformation in complex and demanding environments.

Scaled Agile

Scaled Agile is an approach that aims to extend the principles and practices of Agile methodologies to larger teams and more complex projects. It provides a framework for managing and coordinating the work of multiple Agile teams, allowing them to collaborate and deliver value more effectively at scale.

In the context of Agile process and project management disciplines, Scaled Agile focuses on addressing the challenges that arise when applying Agile principles and practices in larger, more complex environments. Traditional Agile methodologies, such as Scrum, are designed for small, self-organizing teams working on relatively small projects. However, when multiple teams need to collaborate on a larger project, additional coordination and alignment become necessary.

Scaled Agile frameworks, such as SAFe (Scaled Agile Framework), LeSS (Large Scale Scrum), and Nexus, provide guidelines and structures for scaling Agile practices across larger organizations. These frameworks emphasize the importance of alignment, collaboration, and coordination between teams to ensure the overall success of the project.

Scaled Agile also recognizes the need for continuous improvement and adaptability in a dynamic and changing environment. It encourages the use of Agile practices, such as retrospectives and regular feedback loops, to foster a culture of continuous learning and improvement.

Scrum Board

A Scrum board is a visual tool used in Agile Process and Project Management disciplines to track and manage the progress of tasks and work items within a project. It serves as a central information hub for the team, providing a clear and concise overview of the project's status.

The Scrum board typically consists of a physical or digital board divided into columns representing different stages or statuses of the work items. The most common columns are "To Do," "In Progress," and "Done." Each work item, often represented by a sticky note or a card, is moved across the columns as it progresses through the project's workflow.

The primary purpose of the Scrum board is to enhance transparency and visibility. It enables team members and stakeholders to visualize the project's current state, identify any bottlenecks or impediments, and make informed decisions based on real-time information. By having a shared visual representation of the project progress, team members can easily understand what needs to be done, what is currently being worked on, and what has already been completed.

In addition to tracking the progress of work items, the Scrum board also facilitates effective collaboration and communication within the team. It encourages daily stand-up meetings, where team members discuss the tasks they are working on and any obstacles they are facing. This helps to identify and resolve issues promptly, foster collaboration, and align the team's efforts towards achieving project goals.

Scrum Master

A Scrum Master is a key role in the Agile process and project management disciplines. They are responsible for ensuring that the Agile methods and practices are implemented effectively and that the team is able to work efficiently and collaboratively.

The Scrum Master acts as a facilitator and coach for the Agile team, helping to remove any obstacles or barriers to progress. They work closely with the Product Owner to ensure that the requirements and priorities are clear and well-defined, and they also support the team in understanding and following the Agile principles and values.

One of the main responsibilities of the Scrum Master is to promote and support self-organization within the team. They encourage and facilitate open communication and collaboration, fostering a culture of trust and empowerment. They also help to establish and maintain effective Agile ceremonies and processes, such as daily stand-ups, sprint planning, and retrospectives.

The Scrum Master is not a traditional project manager, but rather a servant-leader who enables the team to deliver high-quality results. They focus on ensuring that the Agile team is working towards its goals, removing any impediments along the way. They are also responsible for monitoring and tracking the progress of the project, providing regular feedback and reporting to stakeholders.

In summary, the Scrum Master plays a crucial role in Agile project management, ensuring that the team is able to work effectively and efficiently. They are responsible for removing obstacles, promoting self-organization, and facilitating open communication and collaboration. By doing so, they help to ensure that the Agile team is able to deliver high-quality results and meet their objectives.

Scrum Of Scrums

Scrum of Scrums is a scaled Agile framework that aims to improve coordination and collaboration among multiple Scrum teams working on a large project. It is primarily used in the context of Agile software development for managing complex projects involving multiple teams.

The Scrum of Scrums framework follows the principles of the Scrum methodology and emphasizes the importance of iterative and incremental development. It provides a structured approach for multiple Scrum teams to collaborate and synchronize their work in order to deliver a cohesive and integrated product.

Scrum

Scrum is a framework used in Agile Process and Project Management disciplines. It is an iterative and incremental approach to managing projects, primarily used in software development but also applicable to other complex product development. Scrum focuses on adaptive planning, transparency, and self-organization.

In Scrum, the project is divided into predetermined time frames called sprints. Each sprint typically lasts between one and four weeks. At the beginning of each sprint, a cross-functional team selects a set of prioritized items from the project backlog to work on during the sprint.

During the sprint, the team meets daily in a time-boxed event called the daily scrum or daily stand-up. This is an opportunity for team members to synchronize their work, discuss progress, and identify any impediments. The team collaborates closely, working together to address challenges and meet the sprint goal.

At the end of the sprint, a review meeting is held to demonstrate the work completed to stakeholders. Feedback is gathered, and any necessary adjustments or refinements are made to the project backlog. The team then engages in a retrospective to reflect on the sprint and identify areas for improvement, using this feedback to inform their future work.

One of the key features of Scrum is its emphasis on self-organization. The team is empowered to make decisions and determine how best to achieve the project objectives. This fosters collaboration, creativity, and accountability among team members.

Scrum provides a flexible and adaptable framework for managing projects, allowing for changing priorities and requirements. Its iterative nature enables continuous improvement, delivering value to the customer incrementally throughout the project.

ScrumBan

ScrumBan is an Agile project management framework that combines the principles and practices of both Scrum and Kanban. It aims to provide a flexible approach to managing work and delivering value to the customer.

In ScrumBan, work is organized into iterations or sprints, similar to Scrum. However, the length of these iterations can be more fluid, allowing for more frequent and smaller releases. The work is visualized on a Kanban board, which helps the team to track and manage the flow of work.

ScrumBan emphasizes the importance of continuous improvement and limiting work in progress. This means that the team focuses on completing and delivering one item before moving on to the next. By limiting work in progress, the team can reduce context switching and improve the overall flow of work.

ScrumBan also promotes collaboration and self-organization within the team. The team members are encouraged to work together to plan and prioritize the work, as well as to take ownership of their tasks. This increases transparency and accountability.

Overall, ScrumBan provides a flexible and adaptive approach to project management. It blends the best practices of Scrum and Kanban to enable teams to deliver value incrementally, while continuously improving and streamlining their processes.

ScrumBut

A ScrumBut is a term used in Agile Process and Project Management disciplines to describe a team or organization that claims to follow Scrum practices, but deviates from them in significant ways. It is a combination of the words "Scrum" and "but," signifying that there are various excuses or reasons for not fully embracing Scrum principles.

Scrum is an iterative and incremental Agile framework for managing complex projects. It emphasizes collaboration, flexibility, and adaptability to rapidly deliver value to customers. ScrumButs typically manifest when teams or organizations try to adopt Scrum, but cannot fully commit to its underlying values, principles, and practices.

Some common ScrumButs include:

- "We do Scrum, but we don't have dedicated cross-functional teams." - "We do Scrum, but we don't have a Product Owner." - "We do Scrum, but we don't hold regular ceremonies like Daily Stand-ups or Retrospectives."

These deviations from Scrum practices can impede the team's ability to fully embrace and benefit from the Agile framework, leading to inefficiencies, bottlenecks, and suboptimal results. ScrumButs can emerge due to various reasons, such as organizational resistance to change, lack of understanding of Scrum principles, or the belief that certain practices are not applicable to their specific context.

It is important for teams and organizations to recognize and address their ScrumButs in order to maximize the benefits of Scrum. This can involve providing education and training on Scrum principles, aligning organizational structures and processes with Scrum practices, and fostering a culture of continuous improvement and learning.

Self-Organizing Teams

Self-Organizing Teams, within the context of Agile Process and Project Management disciplines, refer to autonomous groups of individuals who collaborate and coordinate their efforts without explicit direction from a traditional manager or team leader. These teams are empowered to make decisions collectively and have the authority to shape their work processes, responsibilities, and project goals.

Self-organizing teams embrace the principles of Agile methodologies and are central to the success of Agile Software Development. They enable greater flexibility, adaptability, and responsiveness to changing project requirements, thereby promoting efficiency and value delivery. As a result, they foster a sense of ownership and accountability among team members, as they collectively determine how to best achieve the desired outcomes.

Self-organizing teams rely on effective communication, collaboration, and trust among their members. Rather than being directed by a hierarchical authority, team members collaborate and distribute tasks based on their individual skills, expertise, and preferences. Decision-making, problem-solving, and conflict resolution are typically decentralized, promoting a culture of empowerment and continuous improvement.

By allowing self-organizing teams to fully exploit their potential, organizations can harness the collective intelligence and creativity of their members. This fosters innovation, increases team morale, and enhances overall project outcomes. Project managers and leaders, in turn, adopt a supportive role, providing guidance and removing any obstacles that hinder team progress.

Servant Leadership

Servant Leadership in the context of Agile Process and Project Management disciplines refers to a leadership style where the leader prioritizes the needs of their team members and supports them in achieving their goals. It is based on the idea that the leader is a servant to their team, rather than the other way around.

The concept of Servant Leadership aligns well with Agile principles, as it emphasizes collaboration, self-organization, and empowerment. In an Agile project, the Scrum Master or Agile Project Manager acts as a servant leader to the development team, enabling their success by removing obstacles, facilitating effective communication, and ensuring the team has the necessary resources and support to achieve their sprint goals.

Service Blueprint Software

A service blueprint is a tool used in the field of design thinking disciplines to map out and visualize the different components, interactions, and touchpoints that make up a service. It provides a detailed and structured overview of the service delivery process, helping designers and stakeholders understand the user experience and identify areas for improvement.

The service blueprint software enables designers to create and modify service blueprints digitally, making the process more efficient and collaborative. It allows for the creation of visual representations of the service journey, including both front-stage and back-stage activities, customer actions, employee interactions, and supporting processes and systems.

With service blueprint software, designers can easily capture and document the necessary information to assess the effectiveness and efficiency of a service. They can identify pain points, bottlenecks, and opportunities for innovation, which can then inform the design and implementation of new service experiences. By visually mapping out the service journey, designers can gain insights into the customer's perspective, uncovering moments of truth, emotional highs and lows, and areas where the service may fall short of expectations.

Furthermore, the software allows for the collaboration and alignment of different stakeholders involved in the service design process, including designers, business analysts, developers, and managers. It provides a shared platform where teams can work together to analyze, improve, and iterate on the service delivery process, ensuring a seamless and delightful experience for customers.

Service Blueprint

A service blueprint is a visualization tool used in the context of Design Thinking disciplines. It is a detailed representation of the service journey or process, outlining the various interactions and touchpoints between the customer and the service provider.

The service blueprint helps designers and stakeholders understand and map out the entire service experience, from the perspectives of both the customer and the service provider. It aids in identifying pain points, areas of improvement, and opportunities for innovation.

The blueprint consists of different layers or components, including the customer actions, frontstage (visible to the customer) and backstage (invisible to the customer) processes, support processes, physical evidence, and the overall flow of the service journey.

By visualizing the service journey and its underlying components, the blueprint helps teams gain a better understanding of the service ecosystem, uncovering critical touchpoints and potential gaps that may impact the customer experience. It provides insights into the sequence and dependencies of actions, as well as the roles and responsibilities of different stakeholders involved in the service delivery.

Overall, a service blueprint acts as a valuable tool for designers and organizations to design, analyze, and optimize services, ensuring that they meet customer needs and expectations while also considering the feasibility and efficiency of service delivery.

Service Blueprinting Software

A service blueprinting software is a digital tool used to create service blueprints, which are visual representations of the customer journey and the processes and interactions involved in delivering a service. It is designed to support the practice of Design Thinking, a discipline that seeks to understand users' needs and create innovative solutions.

Service blueprinting is a method that helps organizations understand and improve their service offerings by mapping out the entire service journey, from the customer's perspective. It helps to identify touchpoints, pain points, and opportunities for improvement, enabling organizations to provide better experiences for their customers.

The software typically provides a range of features to support the creation of service blueprints, such as drag-and-drop functionality for easily adding and arranging elements, visualization tools for representing different stages of the customer journey, and collaboration features for sharing and collecting feedback from stakeholders.

Service blueprinting software can be a valuable tool for Design Thinking practitioners, as it allows them to quickly and effectively communicate their ideas and insights to team members, stakeholders, and clients. It also enables collaboration and iteration, facilitating the design and improvement of services based on user feedback and input.

Service Blueprints

A service blueprint is a visual representation that outlines the steps and processes involved in delivering a service. It is a tool used in the context of Design Thinking disciplines to understand and improve service experiences.

Service blueprints are created to gain insights into the various touchpoints and interactions between the customer and the service provider. The blueprint helps identify pain points, bottlenecks, and areas of improvement within a service system.

Service Design Blueprints

Service Design Blueprints can be defined as visual representations of the end-to-end journey of a service, outlining all the touchpoints and interactions between the service providers, users, and other stakeholders. It is an essential tool used in the field of Design Thinking to understand, improve, and innovate services.

These blueprints capture both the frontstage and backstage processes involved in delivering a service. They provide a holistic view of the service ecosystem, including physical and digital elements, as well as the people, processes, and systems involved. By mapping out the service journey, designers can identify pain points, inefficiencies, and opportunities for improvement.

Service Design Platforms

Service Design Platforms refer to the digital tools and platforms specifically designed to support and enable the practice of Service Design. Service Design is a multidisciplinary approach that focuses on designing and improving services with a user-centered mindset. It involves understanding the needs and behaviors of users, mapping out the entire service journey, and creating solutions that meet those needs and enhance the overall user experience.

Service Design Platforms are essential in facilitating and streamlining the service design process. They provide a collaborative environment where designers, stakeholders, and users can collaborate, share insights, and co-create service solutions. These platforms typically offer a range of features and functionalities that support different stages of the design process, such as research and insights gathering, ideation and concept development, prototyping and testing, and implementation and evaluation.

The use of Service Design Platforms revolutionizes the design thinking process by making it more accessible, efficient, and effective. They eliminate the need for physical tools and allow for real-time collaboration, remote participation, and global team collaboration. They also enable the collection and analysis of data and feedback, helping designers make more informed decisions and iterate on their solutions.

Ultimately, Service Design Platforms contribute to the democratization of design thinking disciplines by making the process more inclusive and accessible to individuals and organizations. They empower designers to create meaningful and impactful service experiences that meet the evolving needs of users in a fast-paced digital world.

Service Design Thinking

Service design thinking is a discipline within the broader framework of design thinking that focuses specifically on designing and improving services to create better experiences for users and customers. It involves a multidisciplinary approach that combines design, research, and innovation to understand user needs, analyze existing services, and develop new service solutions.

Service design thinking goes beyond merely providing functional and efficient services; it aims to create meaningful experiences and interactions for users at every touchpoint. It considers the entire service journey, from the customer's initial contact with a service provider to their ongoing interaction and eventual departure.

Service Ecosystem Visualization

The service ecosystem visualization is a design thinking discipline that involves the creation of a visual representation of a service system, including all its interconnected elements and relevant stakeholders. It is a tool used to understand and analyze the relationships, interactions, and dependencies within a service ecosystem. This visualization technique helps design thinkers gain a holistic view of the service ecosystem, enabling them to identify opportunities for improvement, anticipate challenges, and innovate new services. It allows stakeholders to visualize the bigger picture and understand how their actions and decisions impact the entire system. The service ecosystem visualization typically consists of a diagram or map that illustrates the various components of the ecosystem, such as customers, service providers, partners, and other relevant entities. It also represents the different touchpoints, channels, and interactions between these components. Design thinkers use this visualization to map out the current state of the service ecosystem and identify pain points, areas of inefficiency, and potential areas for innovation. It helps them uncover hidden relationships, understand the complexity of the system, and identify areas where new services or improvements can be introduced. By visualizing the service ecosystem, design thinkers can better communicate their insights and findings to stakeholders and collaborate on developing solutions. It helps create a shared understanding and a common language for discussing and addressing service-related challenges. In conclusion, the service ecosystem visualization is a design thinking discipline that involves creating a visual representation of a service system. It helps design thinkers understand and analyze the relationships, interactions, and dependencies within the ecosystem, enabling them to identify improvement opportunities and innovate new services.

Service Ecosystems

Service ecosystems refer to the interconnected network of actors, resources, and activities that come together to deliver value through services. In the context of Design Thinking disciplines, service ecosystems play a crucial role in identifying and understanding the various components and interactions that contribute to the design and delivery of a service.

These ecosystems encompass both tangible and intangible elements, including people, organizations, processes, technologies, and physical environments. They are characterized by complex relationships and interdependencies, where each component contributes in its own unique way to the overall service provision and experience.

Design Thinking approaches emphasize the need to thoroughly analyze and map service ecosystems to gain a holistic understanding of the context in which a service operates. This involves identifying and identifying key stakeholders and their roles, mapping out user journeys and touchpoints, and evaluating the impact of different factors on the service delivery process.

By visualizing and analyzing service ecosystems, designers are able to identify pain points, opportunities, and potential areas for innovation. This understanding allows for the development of more user-centric and impactful service solutions, where the needs and preferences of the users are at the center of the design process.

Shippable Increment

A shippable increment is a key concept in Agile project management and development. It refers to a deliverable piece of work that has been completed during a sprint or iteration and is of sufficient quality to be potentially released or deployed to end users.

In the Agile methodology, projects are broken down into smaller, manageable iterations, known as sprints. At the end of each sprint, a shippable increment is produced. This means that the work done during the sprint is brought to a state where it can be considered a potentially releasable product increment.

Short Feedback Loop

A short feedback loop is a critical component of Agile Process and Project Management disciplines. It refers to the continuous and frequent exchange of information and feedback between team members, stakeholders, and customers throughout a project's lifecycle.

In the context of Agile, a short feedback loop enables teams to quickly validate their assumptions and make necessary adjustments to their work. It allows for rapid iterations and incremental improvements, ensuring that the project stays on track and aligned with the desired outcomes. This iterative approach to development promotes adaptability, flexibility, and responsiveness to change.

Simulation

Simulation is a technique used in Agile Project Management to model and replicate real-world scenarios in a controlled environment. It involves creating a virtual representation of a project or process to evaluate its performance, identify potential risks, and make informed decisions.

In Agile Process and Project Management, simulation is employed to assess the impact of various factors such as resource allocation, time constraints, scope changes, and uncertainties on project outcomes. Through the simulation, teams can identify bottlenecks, test different scenarios, and predict the project's overall success or failure. By replicating the project environment, simulation helps teams gain insights into the project's dynamics, dependencies, and critical paths.

One of the key advantages of using simulation in Agile Project Management is its ability to provide a safe and cost-effective platform for experimentation. Instead of making irreversible decisions based on assumptions, teams can use simulation to explore different variables and their potential consequences. This empowers them to make data-driven decisions, mitigating risks and maximizing project success.

The findings from simulations can guide teams in adjusting project specifications, resource allocation, and timelines to optimize outcomes. Simulation also enables teams to anticipate and proactively address potential risks and challenges, improving their ability to adapt and respond quickly during the project's execution.

Social Innovation

Social innovation, in the context of Design Thinking disciplines, refers to the creation of new ideas, products, services, or processes that address social issues and positively impact society. It involves the application of human-centered design principles to identify and solve complex social problems.

Design Thinking, as an iterative and collaborative approach, provides a framework for social innovation by emphasizing empathy, creativity, and prototyping. It begins with a deep understanding of the needs and experiences of the target users or communities through interviews, observations, and immersion in their context. This empathetic understanding serves as a foundation for developing innovative solutions that are user-centric and context-specific.

The process of social innovation within Design Thinking typically involves several stages. First, there is a need identification phase, where researchers and designers gather insights and identify the key challenges faced by individuals or communities. This is followed by an ideation phase, where diverse perspectives are brought together to generate a wide range of potential solutions. These ideas are then prototyped and tested, allowing for quick iterations and refinements based on user feedback.

Importantly, social innovation within Design Thinking also recognizes the importance of collaboration and co-creation. It involves actively involving end-users and stakeholders throughout the design process, ensuring that their voices are heard and their needs are met. This collaborative approach helps to build trust, ownership, and support for the implemented solutions, leading to greater impact and sustainability.

In summary, social innovation in the context of Design Thinking is the practice of applying human-centered design principles to address social challenges, ultimately creating solutions that improve the well-being of individuals and communities.

Social Sustainability

Social sustainability refers to the ability of a society to meet the needs of its current and future generations, while promoting social justice, equity, and inclusivity. In the context of Design Thinking disciplines, social sustainability plays a crucial role in addressing societal and human challenges through empathetic and ethical design practices.

Design Thinking, as an approach to problem-solving, focuses on understanding and empathizing with the needs of users and stakeholders. It encourages a human-centered approach that takes into account the social, cultural, and environmental context in which design solutions operate. Social sustainability adds an important dimension to this approach, ensuring that design solutions not only meet the functional requirements but also consider their impact on people and communities.

Socially Conscious Innovation

Socially Conscious Innovation refers to the application of Design Thinking principles and practices with a focus on creating solutions that address social and environmental challenges. It involves using a human-centered approach to identify and validate social issues, and then developing innovative ideas and strategies to create positive social impact.

This approach recognizes that traditional design and innovation processes may inadvertently contribute to or perpetuate social problems, and aims to shift the focus towards creating solutions that are not only economically viable but also promote social equality, ecological sustainability, and overall well-being of communities.

Socially Impactful Design

Socially Impactful Design can be defined as the application of design thinking principles and methodologies to create solutions that address social problems, drive positive change, and improve the overall well-being of individuals and communities.

Design Thinking is a problem-solving approach that focuses on empathy, user-centeredness, and collaboration. It involves understanding the needs and aspirations of people, generating creative ideas, and developing innovative solutions. When applied to social issues, Design Thinking can help identify and address complex challenges in areas such as healthcare, education, poverty, environmental sustainability, and access to basic resources.

Solution Exploration

Design Thinking is a problem-solving approach that applies principles and methodologies from design disciplines to address complex challenges and create innovative solutions. It is a human-centered and iterative process that aims to understand users' needs, redefine problems, and generate creative ideas to meet those needs.

At its core, Design Thinking involves five interconnected and non-linear stages: empathize, define, ideate, prototype, and test. These stages allow a multidisciplinary team to deeply understand the users and their contexts, define the problem statement, brainstorm and explore a wide range of possible solutions, build and iterate on physical or digital prototypes, and gather feedback through testing and observation.

Empathizing is about developing a deep understanding of users, their motivations, and their pain points through observation, interviews, and immersive experiences. Defining involves synthesizing the gathered information, identifying patterns, and framing the problem statement in a human-centered way. Ideating encourages the generation of a diverse range of ideas and encourages wild and unconventional thinking. Prototyping allows teams to translate ideas into tangible artifacts, which can be further refined and improved through iteration. Finally, testing involves collecting feedback from users to validate assumptions, uncover new insights, and inform the next iteration of the design.

Design Thinking encourages collaboration, prototyping, and experimentation to refine solutions and discover new possibilities. It embraces ambiguity and uncertainty, promoting a mindset of constant learning and iteration. By focusing on the needs and motivations of users, Design Thinking aims to create innovative, useful, and meaningful solutions that can meet real-world challenges.

In summary, Design Thinking leverages design principles and methodologies to approach problem-solving in a holistic, human-centered, and iterative way. It combines empathy, collaboration, and creativity to redefine problems, generate ideas, build prototypes, and test solutions in order to create innovative and impactful outcomes.

Solution Ideation

Design Thinking is a problem-solving approach that focuses on understanding the needs and preferences of users in order to create effective and innovative solutions. It encompasses a variety of disciplines that contribute to the overall process of designing and developing products, services, or experiences.

These disciplines include:

1. Empathy: This involves gaining a deep understanding of the target audience and their needs, desires, and motivations. Design thinkers use various tools and techniques such as interviews, observations, and surveys to gather insights and develop a sense of empathy with the users. 2. Defining the problem: Once a thorough understanding of the users is achieved, the next step is to define the problem or challenge that needs to be addressed. This involves framing the problem in a way that is user-centered and actionable. The problem statement should be concise, clear, and focused. 3. Ideation: This is the phase where creative ideas and solutions are generated. Design thinkers use brainstorming sessions and other ideation techniques to encourage wild and innovative thinking. The aim is to generate a wide range of ideas without judgment or criticism. 4. Prototyping: After selecting the most promising ideas, the design team creates prototypes or representations of the proposed solutions. Prototypes can take various forms such as physical models, wireframes, or simulations. These prototypes are used to gather feedback and make necessary improvements. 5. Testing and iterating: The prototypes are tested with the users to evaluate their effectiveness and gather feedback. Based on the feedback, the design team iterates and refines the solutions to make them more user-friendly and aligned with the needs and preferences of the target audience. Design Thinking is an iterative and collaborative approach that encourages cross-disciplinary collaboration and a deep understanding of the user. It aims to create meaningful and impactful solutions by putting the user at the center of the design process.

Solution Space

The solution space refers to the range of potential solutions that are generated during the design thinking process. It is an exploratory phase where designers and problem solvers aim to identify innovative and effective solutions to a specific problem or challenge.

During the solution space phase, designers engage in rapid ideation and brainstorming to generate as many solutions as possible. This divergent thinking approach encourages creativity and the exploration of unconventional ideas. The goal is to move beyond obvious or predictable solutions and explore innovative possibilities.

Once a wide range of potential solutions has been generated, designers then begin to narrow down the options through convergent thinking. They evaluate each solution in terms of feasibility, desirability, and viability. This involves considering factors such as technical constraints, user needs, business goals, and resource availability.

The solution space is not limited to a single "right" answer. Instead, it encompasses a spectrum of potential solutions, each with its own strengths and weaknesses. Designers must carefully weigh the trade-offs and make informed decisions about which solutions to develop further.

The solution space often requires an iterative approach, as designers may need to revisit and refine their ideas based on user feedback, testing, and iteration. It is through this process of exploration and iteration that the most innovative and effective solutions emerge.

Spaghetti Diagram

A spaghetti diagram is a visual representation that illustrates the flow of people, materials, or information within a process or system. It is typically used in the context of Agile Process and Project Management disciplines to identify and eliminate waste, reduce inefficiencies, and improve overall productivity.

The diagram gets its name from its resemblance to a plate of spaghetti, with multiple lines zigzagging and intertwining to represent the movement and interactions of different elements in the process. By plotting the actual paths and steps taken by individuals or items, the spaghetti diagram provides a comprehensive and objective view of the process, enabling teams to identify bottlenecks, congestion, and unnecessary movements.

In Agile Process and Project Management, the spaghetti diagram serves as a valuable tool for process analysis, continuous improvement, and waste reduction. By visually mapping the current state of a process, teams can identify areas for optimization and implement changes to streamline workflows and eliminate non-value-added activities.

The spaghetti diagram can also be used to identify opportunities for automation, standardization, and simplification. It helps teams to visualize the physical layout and arrangement of workstations, equipment, and resources, allowing them to make informed decisions on reorganizing the workspace to minimize movement and improve efficiency.

Speculative Prototyping

Speculative Prototyping is a technique used within the Design Thinking discipline to explore and validate alternative ideas and potential solutions. It involves quickly creating and testing low-fidelity prototypes to gather feedback and generate insights that inform the design process.

The aim of Speculative Prototyping is to push the boundaries of traditional problem-solving by introducing creativity and imagination into the design process. By creating prototypes that may seem unconventional or speculative, designers can challenge assumptions, engage users in new ways, and uncover unique opportunities for innovation.

Sprint Backlog

Sprint Backlog is a dynamic list of prioritized user stories or tasks that are planned to be completed during a sprint in the Agile process. It is an essential artifact used in Agile project management disciplines to track and manage the progress of work within a sprint.

The Sprint Backlog is created during the Sprint Planning meeting, where the Scrum team collaboratively selects the highest-priority items from the Product Backlog and commits to completing them within the fixed time frame of the sprint. The selected items are broken down into smaller, manageable tasks, which are then added to the Sprint Backlog.

The Sprint Backlog serves as a tool for the Scrum team to plan their work and ensure transparency and accountability throughout the sprint. It helps the team to stay focused on the work they have committed to complete and provides a visual representation of the tasks that need to be accomplished.

During the sprint, the Sprint Backlog is used by the team to track their progress, update the status of tasks, and identify any obstacles or dependencies that may impact the timely completion of work. The team holds daily stand-up meetings to discuss the status of tasks and to collaborate on resolving any issues or impediments.

At the end of the sprint, the Sprint Backlog is reviewed and the completed work is demonstrated to the stakeholders. Any unfinished work is either carried forward to the next sprint or reprioritized in the Product Backlog.

Sprint Goal

A Sprint Goal in the context of Agile Process and Project Management disciplines is a concise statement that describes the objective or outcome that the Agile team aims to achieve by the end of a sprint.

It serves as a guiding principle for the team and provides a clear focus for their work during the sprint. The Sprint Goal helps the team prioritize their tasks and make decisions based on what will contribute most effectively to the achievement of the goal.

The Sprint Goal is determined collaboratively by the Agile team, including the Product Owner and the Scrum Master, during the Sprint Planning meeting. It is based on the priorities set by the Product Owner and the understanding of the work required to deliver a valuable increment of the product.

By having a Sprint Goal, the team can align their efforts and have a shared understanding of what needs to be achieved. It also helps in identifying potential scope changes during the sprint that may conflict with the goal, allowing the team to assess the impact and make informed decisions.

The Sprint Goal is used as a measure of success at the end of the sprint. If the goal is met, it indicates that the team has delivered the intended value. If not, it becomes a valuable learning opportunity for the team to reflect on the obstacles faced and adjust their approach in subsequent sprints.

Sprint Planning

Sprint Planning is a key event in Agile Process and Project Management disciplines. It is a collaborative meeting that involves the Scrum Team, consisting of the Product Owner, Scrum Master, and the development team. The primary objective of Sprint Planning is to determine the work that will be completed during the upcoming sprint.

During Sprint Planning, the Product Owner discusses the highest-priority user stories or product backlog items with the team. The team clarifies any doubts or questions they have regarding the product backlog items. The Product Owner then selects the items that will be part of the upcoming sprint, based on the team's capacity and velocity.

Once the selection is made, the team collectively decomposes the selected items into smaller tasks. Each task is estimated in terms of effort required for completion. This estimation helps in determining the sprint backlog and creating a realistic plan for the sprint.

During Sprint Planning, the Scrum Team also sets a sprint goal, which serves as a unifying objective for the team to work towards. The team also discusses and defines the acceptance criteria for each selected item to ensure a common understanding of the expected outcome.

Sprint Planning typically has a time-boxed duration, with the recommended guideline being one hour for every week of the sprint. The outcome of the Sprint Planning is a well-defined sprint backlog that contains the selected product backlog items, corresponding tasks, estimates, and the sprint goal.

Sprint Review

A Sprint Review is a key ceremony in the Agile process and an integral component of project management disciplines. It serves as a formal gathering for the Agile team, stakeholders, and customers to assess the progress made during the sprint and gather feedback for future improvements.

During the Sprint Review, the Scrum team demonstrates the completed work items to the stakeholders, showcasing the value delivered during the sprint. The team presents the product increment, highlighting the features that have been implemented and the user stories that have been completed. This demonstration facilitates open communication and transparency among the team and stakeholders.

The Sprint Review also allows stakeholders and customers to provide valuable feedback on the implemented features, user experience, and overall product direction. This feedback helps the team understand the stakeholders' needs, identify areas for improvement, and make necessary adjustments to the product backlog or future sprints.

Additionally, the Sprint Review provides an opportunity for the stakeholders and customers to re-prioritize the product backlog based on the feedback received during the review. This ensures that the product development remains aligned with the evolving needs of the stakeholders and maximizes the value delivered to the end-users.

In summary, the Sprint Review is a crucial ceremony in the Agile process and project management disciplines. It promotes collaboration, transparency, and continuous improvement by facilitating the demonstration of completed work, gathering feedback from stakeholders, and reassessing the product backlog and priorities.

Sprint

A sprint is a time-boxed iteration of work in the Agile Process and Project Management disciplines. It is a fixed period of time, typically ranging from one to four weeks, during which a specific set of tasks, user stories, or features are planned, designed, developed, and tested.

Sprints are a key component of the Agile methodology, which emphasizes iterative and incremental development. They allow teams to break their work into manageable chunks and deliver value to stakeholders more frequently. Each sprint is planned in advance and has a defined goal or objective, which is often represented by a set of user stories or requirements.

Stakeholder Collaboration

Stakeholder Collaboration, within the context of Design Thinking disciplines, refers to the process of actively involving and engaging various stakeholders in the design and decision-making process. This collaborative approach aims to gather different perspectives, insights, and expertise to enhance the overall design solution and ensure its alignment with the needs and expectations of all stakeholders involved.

By fostering stakeholder collaboration, designers and teams can leverage the collective knowledge and experiences of different individuals or groups to generate a more comprehensive understanding of the problem or challenge at hand. This collaborative environment encourages open communication, empathy, and the exploration of diverse ideas and perspectives, ultimately leading to innovative and impactful design outcomes.

Stakeholder Engagement Platforms

Stakeholder Engagement Platforms, within the context of Design Thinking disciplines, refer to digital tools or platforms that facilitate the active involvement and collaboration of stakeholders throughout the design process. These platforms serve as virtual spaces where stakeholders can effectively engage, interact, and contribute to the design process, while also providing a means to gather and collect valuable insights and feedback.

Stakeholder Engagement Platforms enable designers to create a more inclusive and participatory design process by ensuring that the perspectives, needs, and desires of all stakeholders are considered. They provide a structured framework for stakeholders to share their ideas, opinions, and concerns, as well as to co-create and collaborate on design concepts, prototypes, and solutions.

Stakeholder Engagement

Stakeholder Engagement, in the context of Agile Process and Project Management disciplines, refers to the intentional and active involvement of individuals or groups who have an interest in or will be affected by a project. It is a critical component of successful project delivery as it ensures that all relevant stakeholders are identified, understood, and engaged throughout the project lifecycle.

The Agile approach emphasizes ongoing collaboration with stakeholders, recognizing that their input is valuable in shaping the project's direction and maximizing its value. Stakeholder Engagement involves not only gathering requirements and feedback but also fostering open lines of communication, building relationships, and promoting shared ownership of project outcomes.

Effective Stakeholder Engagement requires a systematic and iterative approach, aligned with Agile principles. This involves identifying and prioritizing stakeholders based on their influence, power, and interest in the project. Regular and continuous engagement activities, such as meetings, workshops, and reviews, are conducted to gather insights, validate assumptions, and gain consensus on key decisions.

Stakeholder Engagement in Agile projects goes beyond traditional project management practices by promoting flexibility, adaptability, and responsiveness to stakeholder needs and expectations. It provides stakeholders with frequent opportunities to provide input, review project progress, and provide feedback on deliverables.

By actively involving stakeholders throughout the project, Agile teams can ensure that their solutions are aligned with business objectives, meet user needs, and address potential issues or risks. This collaborative approach not only improves project outcomes but also enhances stakeholder satisfaction and engagement, ultimately contributing to the overall success of the project.

Stakeholder

A stakeholder, in the context of Agile Process and Project Management disciplines, refers to an individual, group, or organization that has a vested interest or a significant impact on a project or initiative. They are the people or entities that have the potential to affect or be affected by the project's outcomes, deliverables, or decisions.

Stakeholders play a crucial role in Agile processes as they provide the necessary input and feedback throughout the project lifecycle. They are involved in various stages, from defining requirements to testing the final product, ensuring that their needs and expectations are considered.

Story Points

Story Points are a unit of measure used in Agile project management to estimate the effort required to complete a task or User Story. They help the development team to determine the complexity and scope of the work to be done, and provide a basis for planning and prioritizing tasks.

In Agile, projects are divided into smaller, manageable chunks called User Stories. These stories represent the requirements or features that need to be delivered. Instead of estimating the time it will take to complete a task, the team estimates the relative effort or complexity using Story Points. This allows for more flexibility and adaptability in the planning process.

Story Points are usually based on a scale determined by the team, typically ranging from 1 to 20 or more. The scale is not linear, meaning that a task with 5 Story Points is not necessarily twice as complex as a task with 2 Story Points. Instead, the scale represents a relative measure of effort based on the team's collective knowledge and experience.

Using Story Points allows the team to focus on the complexity and effort required for a task, rather than getting caught up in the specifics of how long it will take. This helps to remove biases and assumptions about individual team members' productivity and allows for more accurate and consistent estimation.

Strategic Design Thinking

Strategic Design Thinking is a discipline within the broader context of Design Thinking that focuses on aligning design processes with strategic goals and objectives. It combines creative problem solving methods with strategic planning frameworks to generate innovative solutions that effectively address complex business challenges.

At its core, Strategic Design Thinking involves an iterative and collaborative approach that encourages cross-functional teams to explore and prototype different ideas, concepts, and prototypes. This mindset enables organizations to generate breakthrough solutions that meet the needs of both the business and its end users or customers.

Strategic Design

Strategic Design is a crucial aspect of Design Thinking that encompasses the application of long-term planning and forward-thinking approaches to the design process. It focuses on creating solutions that align with an organization's goals and objectives, taking into account the broader context and potential future challenges.

By integrating strategic thinking into the design process, organizations can develop innovative and sustainable solutions that address complex problems effectively. Strategic Design involves conducting extensive research, analyzing data, and understanding user needs to ultimately inform the design decisions.

Strategic Foresight

Strategic Foresight is a discipline within Design Thinking that involves the exploration and analysis of potential futures to inform strategic decision-making. It seeks to identify emerging trends, uncertainties, and opportunities that could shape the business landscape and impact design outcomes.

Through collaborative and interdisciplinary approaches, Strategic Foresight allows designers and organizations to anticipate and prepare for possible future scenarios. It goes beyond traditional forecasting methods by considering various factors such as social, technological, economic, environmental, and political changes that could influence design choices.

Sustainable Materials

Sustainable materials are those that are produced, used, and disposed of in a manner that minimizes negative environmental impacts and supports the long-term well-being of people and the planet. In the context of design thinking disciplines, sustainable materials are considered a crucial component in creating innovative and eco-friendly solutions.

Design thinking is an approach that emphasizes empathy, collaboration, and iterative problem-solving to address complex challenges. When applying design thinking principles to sustainable materials, designers seek to identify materials that have a lower carbon footprint, reduce waste, conserve resources, and promote social equity.

Swarming

Swarming is a collaborative approach used in Agile Process and Project Management disciplines to address complex tasks or projects. It refers to the practice of having multiple team members work together simultaneously on the same task or set of tasks, with the goal of accelerating progress and improving efficiency.

In a swarming approach, the team organizes itself around the task at hand, rather than assigning individual responsibilities. Team members come together, share their skills and knowledge, and collaborate closely to complete the work as quickly and effectively as possible. This allows for faster decision-making, improved problem-solving, and increased adaptability to changing circumstances.

Synthesis

Design Thinking is a problem-solving approach that incorporates empathy, experimentation, and collaboration to generate innovative solutions. It is a discipline that combines analytical and creative thinking to tackle complex challenges, with the ultimate goal of improving the user experience.

At its core, Design Thinking is driven by a deep understanding of users' needs and motivations. It involves conducting research, interviews, and observations to gain insights into user behavior and preferences. By putting themselves in the users' shoes, designers empathize with their pain points and strive to address them effectively.

The next step in the Design Thinking process is ideation, where designers brainstorm and generate a wide range of ideas. This phase encourages divergent thinking and embraces creativity without judgment. By considering multiple perspectives and reframing problems, designers can unlock innovative solutions that may have been overlooked initially.

Once a pool of ideas is generated, prototypes are created to test and refine them. This experimental approach allows designers to gather feedback, iterate, and improve their concepts. Through rapid prototyping and user testing, designers can identify what works and what doesn't, leading to informed decision-making.

Collaboration is a fundamental aspect of Design Thinking. Cross-functional teams with diverse backgrounds and expertise come together to contribute their unique perspectives and skills. This multidisciplinary approach fosters collaboration, knowledge sharing, and iterative co-creation.

In conclusion, Design Thinking is a human-centered problem-solving methodology that combines empathy, ideation, prototyping, and collaboration. It is not constrained to a specific industry or context, as it can be applied to any problem that requires innovative solutions and engenders a positive user experience.

System Thinking

System Thinking is a crucial component of Design Thinking disciplines that involves a holistic approach to understanding and solving complex problems. It focuses on comprehending the interdependencies and relationships within a system, rather than isolating individual components.

By viewing a problem as part of a larger system, System Thinking aims to uncover the underlying structures, patterns, and dynamics that shape the behavior of the system. This approach allows designers to identify the root causes of issues and develop effective strategies that address the system as a whole, rather than merely addressing symptoms or superficial aspects.

Systemic Design

Systemic Design is a discipline within Design Thinking that aims to understand and solve complex problems by considering the interconnected components and relationships within a system. It focuses on the systemic nature of the problem, rather than viewing it in isolation.

Systemic Design recognizes that a problem cannot be fully understood or solved by solely examining its individual parts. Instead, it emphasizes the need to understand the connections, interactions, and dependencies between these parts. By doing so, it seeks to identify patterns, feedback loops, and unintended consequences that may emerge within the system.

Through a holistic approach, Systemic Design encourages designers to consider the broader context in which a problem exists. This includes societal, economic, cultural, and environmental factors that may influence the problem and potential solutions. By taking into account a wide range of perspectives and stakeholders, Systemic Design aims to create solutions that are more inclusive and sustainable.

Systemic Design also emphasizes the iterative and collaborative nature of the design process. It encourages designers to engage with stakeholders throughout all stages of the design process, fostering co-creation and shared ownership of the problem and solution. This helps to ensure that the solution is not only technically feasible but also socially acceptable and culturally appropriate.

Systemic Innovation

Systemic Innovation refers to a multidisciplinary approach within Design Thinking that aims to create transformative change in complex systems. It involves reimagining and redesigning entire systems rather than focusing on isolated elements or components.

This approach recognizes that problems and challenges are often interconnected and cannot be effectively addressed through traditional linear thinking. Systemic Innovation seeks to understand the underlying dynamics and relationships within a system and identify opportunities for intervention and improvement.

Systemic Problem Solving

Systemic Problem Solving refers to the approach employed within the framework of Design Thinking disciplines to address complex issues and challenges in a holistic and comprehensive manner. It involves identifying and understanding the root causes of the problem, exploring multiple perspectives, and developing solutions that are sustainable and have a positive impact on the entire system.

This problem-solving methodology acknowledges that problems rarely exist in isolation, but are interconnected and influenced by various factors within a system. By taking a systemic view, designers can effectively analyze the relationships, interdependencies, and feedback loops within the system to identify leverage points for intervention.

Systemic Thinking

Systemic thinking, within the context of Design Thinking disciplines, refers to the practice of understanding and addressing complex problems by considering the larger systems and interconnectedness involved.

It involves recognizing that any problem or challenge exists within a broader context, and that various elements within the system are interdependent and influence each other. Rather than focusing on isolated parts or symptoms, systemic thinking aims to identify the underlying patterns, relationships, and dynamics that shape the problem.

Systems Thinking

Systems Thinking is an interdisciplinary approach that recognizes and investigates the complex interactions and interdependencies within a system. It involves understanding the different components of a system, how they interact with one another, and the impact of these interactions on the overall system behavior. In the context of Design Thinking disciplines, Systems Thinking refers to the ability to analyze and comprehend the interconnectedness between various elements of a design problem.

Designers practicing Systems Thinking strive to identify the relationships, patterns, and feedback loops that exist within a system. They consider the implications of changes made to one part of a system on other parts, as well as the system as a whole. By taking a holistic perspective, they aim to anticipate potential unintended consequences and design solutions that address the underlying complexities of the system.

T-Shirt Sizing

The term "T-shirt sizing" refers to a high-level estimation technique used in Agile Process and Project Management disciplines to forecast, plan, and prioritize work items or user stories. It is based on the analogy of assigning sizes to t-shirts, such as Small, Medium, Large, or Extra Large, to represent the effort or complexity associated with each work item.

T-shirt sizing is a quick and simplified approach that allows project teams to gain a common understanding of the relative effort and complexity of different work items. It aids in prioritization, resource allocation, and capacity planning by providing a rough indication of the amount of work involved in implementing each item.

During the t-shirt sizing process, the project team collectively assesses the work items and assigns a size to each based on their expert judgment and experience. This assessment is typically done in a collaborative session or workshop, where team members discuss and debate the characteristics and dependencies of the items. The goal is to reach a consensus and establish a shared understanding of the relative sizes of the work items.

T-shirt sizing does not focus on precise estimates or hours of effort, but rather on creating a relative sizing scale. It helps to identify the most complex or time-consuming work items, which can then be further broken down into smaller, more manageable tasks for detailed estimation and planning.

In summary, t-shirt sizing is a high-level estimation technique that allows project teams to quickly assess and prioritize work items based on their relative effort and complexity. It facilitates effective resource allocation, capacity planning, and prioritization in Agile Process and Project Management disciplines.

Task Board

A Task Board is a visual representation of the work that needs to be done for a project, in the context of Agile Process and Project Management disciplines. It is a commonly used tool in Agile methodologies, such as Scrum, to track and manage the progress of tasks throughout the project lifecycle.

The Task Board typically consists of a physical or digital board divided into columns that represent different stages of work, such as "To Do," "In Progress," and "Done." Each task is represented by a sticky note or card that contains relevant information, such as the task description, owner, and status. The tasks are visually moved across the columns as they progress from one stage to another.

The Task Board provides several benefits to the Agile project team. First, it serves as a central hub for all team members to easily access and understand the current state of the project. It promotes transparency and collaborative decision-making. Second, it helps the team prioritize work by providing a clear visual representation of the tasks at hand. Prioritization is typically achieved by assigning color codes or tags to tasks based on their importance or urgency. Third, it facilitates effective communication within the team, as team members can quickly see who is working on what and identify potential bottlenecks or dependencies. Finally, the Task Board enables the team to visualize and measure their progress over time, which can be helpful for retrospectives and continuous improvement.

Technical Debt

Technical Debt refers to the concept in Agile Process and Project Management disciplines which refers to the accumulation of incomplete, inefficient, or poorly implemented code or design in a software project. It represents the shortcuts taken or compromises made during development that result in a suboptimal or less maintainable product.

Unlike financial debt, technical debt is not just a matter of time and effort required to pay it off. It also carries the risk of negatively impacting future development and maintenance efforts. Just like debt accrues interest, technical debt accumulates additional costs and complexities over time. It can lead to longer development cycles, increased bug rates, and decreased system stability.

There are various causes of technical debt, such as deadline pressure, lack of technical expertise, insufficient resources, or changing requirements. It is important for Agile teams and project managers to address technical debt proactively and prevent it from accumulating. This may involve refactoring or rewriting code, improving documentation, or allocating additional resources to fix existing issues.

In order to manage technical debt effectively, Agile teams prioritize and plan technical debt repayment alongside new feature development. Team members are encouraged to improve the codebase incrementally and take collective ownership of the debt. By acknowledging and addressing technical debt in a timely manner, organizations can ensure that they can continue to deliver high-quality software products that are sustainable and adaptable in the long term.

Technical Excellence

Technical Excellence is a key principle in Agile Process and Project Management disciplines. It encompasses the high-quality execution of development activities and the continuous improvement of technical skills and practices within a team.

Technical Excellence aims to deliver value to the customer by ensuring that the software being developed is of the highest possible quality. It involves following best practices, adhering to coding standards, and employing techniques such as test-driven development and continuous integration. By doing so, the team can minimize defects, reduce technical debt, and deliver a reliable and maintainable product.

Technical Excellence also emphasizes the importance of continuous learning and refining technical skills. Agile teams regularly reflect on their work, identifying areas for improvement and investing time in honing their craft. This includes staying up to date with new technologies, attending training sessions or conferences, and seeking feedback from peers.

In addition, collaboration and knowledge sharing are vital aspects of Technical Excellence. Agile teams encourage open communication, pair programming, and code reviews to foster a learning culture. By working together and leveraging each other's expertise, the team can produce higher quality code and make better-informed decisions.

Ultimately, Technical Excellence enables Agile teams to continuously deliver valuable software that meets or exceeds customer expectations. It ensures that the software is well-architected, reliable, and easily maintainable while fostering a learning mindset within the team.

Technology Adoption

Technology adoption, in the context of Design Thinking disciplines, refers to the process of integrating new technologies or innovations into the design and development of products, services, or experiences. It involves the conscious decision and acceptance of incorporating new technologies in order to enhance and improve the overall design solution.

Design Thinking disciplines emphasize the importance of empathizing with users, defining their needs, ideating potential solutions, prototyping and testing them, and finally implementing the most appropriate design solution. Technology adoption plays a crucial role in this process as it enables designers to create designs that effectively address user needs and provide innovative solutions.

Technology Integration

Technology integration in the context of Design Thinking disciplines refers to the intentional and strategic incorporation of technology tools and resources into the various stages of the design process. This integration aims to enhance the design thinking approach by leveraging the capabilities of technology to improve problem-solving, creativity, and collaboration.

By integrating technology into design thinking, practitioners can access a wide range of digital tools that enable them to gather and analyze data, visualize ideas, prototype and test solutions, and share their work with stakeholders. These tools can include software applications, virtual reality environments, data collection devices, and communication platforms, among others.

Test Automation

Test Automation is a process in Agile Project Management that involves utilizing software tools and frameworks to automatically execute and manage test cases. It aims to increase the efficiency and reliability of software testing by reducing the manual effort required for repetitive tasks.

In an Agile context, Test Automation plays a vital role in achieving the iterative and fast-paced nature of software development. It allows for continuous integration and delivery by enabling tests to be executed frequently and consistently. By automating the execution of test cases, Agile teams can quickly identify any defects or issues, allowing for immediate feedback and rectification.

Through the use of test automation tools, Agile Project Management disciplines can track and monitor the progress and quality of the software being developed. These tools provide metrics and reports that help measure the effectiveness and coverage of the automated tests. This information enables project managers to make informed decisions regarding the software's readiness for release.

Test Automation also enhances collaboration within Agile teams by providing a shared platform for test planning, execution, and reporting. It facilitates effective communication between developers, testers, and other stakeholders, ensuring a shared understanding of the software's functionality and requirements.

In summary, Test Automation in Agile Project Management is the practice of using software tools and frameworks to automate the execution and management of test cases. It enables Agile teams to enhance the efficiency, reliability, and quality of software testing, supporting the iterative and fast-paced nature of Agile development.

Test And Learn

Test and Learn is a fundamental principle in the discipline of Design Thinking, which is an iterative and user-focused approach to problem-solving. It refers to the continuous process of testing ideas, solutions, and prototypes in order to gain feedback, validate assumptions, and make improvements.

Test and Learn involves conducting experiments, gathering data, and analyzing results to inform the design and development of a product, service, or experience. This iterative process allows designers to refine their concepts and address any issues or challenges that may arise, ultimately leading to more effective and user-centric solutions.

Test-Driven Development (TDD)

Test-Driven Development (TDD), in the context of Agile Process and Project Management disciplines, is an iterative software development approach that emphasizes the creation of automated tests before implementing the actual code. This practice enables teams to continuously validate the software's functionality and detect defects or inconsistencies early in the development process.

TDD follows a specific cycle, known as the Red-Green-Refactor cycle, which involves three steps: writing failing tests (Red), writing the minimum amount of code required to pass the tests (Green), and improving the code without changing its functionality (Refactor). By following this cycle, TDD promotes the production of high-quality code in short iterations.

Theme

Agile Process: Agile process is a project management approach that emphasizes flexibility, collaboration, and continuous improvement in order to deliver high-quality results. It is based on the principles outlined in the Agile Manifesto, which values individuals and interactions, working software, customer collaboration, and responding to change.

Agile processes are iterative and incremental, allowing for frequent feedback and adaptation. Instead of following a rigid, linear plan, Agile teams work in short time-boxed iterations called sprints, where they prioritize and deliver small pieces of value. This iterative approach helps to mitigate risks, manage changing requirements, and ensure that the project is aligning with the customer's needs.

The Agile process is characterized by its emphasis on self-organizing teams and close collaboration between team members. Communication is highly valued, with team members regularly discussing progress, challenges, and potential solutions. This promotes transparency and helps the team stay aligned and focused on achieving the project goals.

Agile Process Management: Agile process management refers to the practices and techniques used to effectively plan, monitor, and control Agile projects. It involves the application of Agile principles to ensure that the project is progressing smoothly, resources are properly allocated, and risks are identified and addressed.

Agile process management involves frequent and transparent communication within the Agile team and with stakeholders. It requires the use of Agile project management tools and techniques, such as user stories, prioritization techniques, and sprint planning. By closely monitoring progress and adapting as necessary, Agile process management ensures that the project remains on track and continues to deliver value to the customer.

Time-To-Market

Time-to-Market is a critical measure in the Agile process and Project Management disciplines, referring to the amount of time it takes for a product or feature to be developed, tested, and made available to customers in the market.

Agile methodologies, such as Scrum, emphasize reducing the Time-to-Market by delivering incremental value frequently and early in the project lifecycle. By breaking down a project into small, manageable pieces called sprints, Agile teams can prioritize the most valuable features and ensure they are delivered quickly. This iterative approach allows for continuous feedback and ensures that the product can be adjusted based on customer needs and market demands throughout the development process.

Timebox

Timeboxing is a technique used in Agile Process and Project Management disciplines to define and limit the amount of time that will be allocated to a specific task or activity. It involves setting a fixed time duration for a task, and ensuring that all efforts are focused on completing the task within that time constraint.

The main purpose of timeboxing is to create a sense of urgency and promote efficiency in completing tasks. By setting strict time limits, the team is encouraged to prioritize their work, make quick decisions, and avoid getting bogged down in unnecessary details. It helps to prevent scope creep and encourages a disciplined and focused approach to achieving project goals.

Timeboxing

Timeboxing is a time management technique utilized in Agile Process and Project Management disciplines. It involves allocating a fixed amount of time for a specific task or activity, and ensuring that it is completed within that timeframe. The main objective of timeboxing is to increase productivity and focus by setting clear time boundaries and preventing tasks from expanding beyond their intended scope.

In Agile Process and Project Management, timeboxing is often used in conjunction with iterative and incremental development approaches. It allows teams to work on small, manageable chunks of work called timeboxes or time intervals, typically ranging from a few hours to a few weeks. During each timebox, the team focuses on delivering a specific set of features or completing a pre-defined task, with the aim of producing a potentially shippable product

101

increment.

Timeboxing helps facilitate collaboration and decision-making within the team. It encourages team members to prioritize, plan, and execute their work more effectively, as they are aware of the fixed time constraint. By having regular timeboxes, Agile teams can also incorporate feedback and adapt their approach based on changing requirements or market conditions.

Overall, timeboxing is a valuable tool in Agile Process and Project Management as it promotes efficiency and accountability. It helps teams stay on track, maintain a steady pace of progress, and meet delivery deadlines successfully. By breaking down work into manageable units, timeboxing allows for more accurate estimation of time and effort required, providing a foundation for better planning and resource allocation.

Tolerance For Failure

Tolerance for Failure is an essential concept within the discipline of Design Thinking. It refers to the willingness and acceptance of experiencing failures or setbacks during the creative and problem-solving process without becoming discouraged or deterred.

Design Thinking encourages professionals to embrace failures as learning opportunities and stepping stones towards innovative solutions. By adopting a mindset of tolerance for failure, practitioners can foster creativity, take risks, and explore unconventional ideas without fear of being wrong or making mistakes.

Transdisciplinary

Transdisciplinary in the context of Design Thinking disciplines refers to the integration and collaboration of multiple disciplines or fields of knowledge to solve complex problems and create innovative solutions. It goes beyond a multidisciplinary approach, which involves bringing different disciplines together, and instead focuses on the synthesis and co-creation of knowledge across disciplines.

In a transdisciplinary approach, professionals with diverse expertise, such as designers, engineers, psychologists, sociologists, and business strategists, work together to understand the problem from various perspectives and develop a holistic understanding of the context. This collaborative effort allows for the exploration of different angles, the identification of interrelationships, and the discovery of unique insights and opportunities that may not be apparent in a single disciplinary approach.

Transformational Design

Transformational Design is a concept rooted in the principles of Design Thinking, which is a human-centered approach to problem-solving and innovation. It is a discipline that focuses on creating meaningful and positive changes in individuals, organizations, and society as a whole.

Transformational Design incorporates empathy, creativity, and collaboration to identify and address complex challenges, in order to bring about transformation and improvement. It goes beyond just creating aesthetically pleasing designs, and instead seeks to understand people's needs, desires, and aspirations, and design solutions that can have a profound impact on their lives.

Transformational Solutions

Transformational Solutions in the context of Design Thinking disciplines refer to innovative and forward-thinking strategies and approaches that aim to address complex problems and create positive change. It involves a deep understanding of the problem at hand and focuses on designing solutions that have the potential to transform current practices, systems, and behaviors.

Design Thinking, as a problem-solving methodology, encompasses various stages, including empathizing, defining the problem, ideating, prototyping, and testing. Transformational Solutions are outcomes that arise from this iterative process, where designers aim to challenge the status quo and create new and improved ways of doing things.

Transformative Design

Transformative Design is a concept that lies at the intersection of Design Thinking disciplines. It refers to the process of creating innovative and impactful solutions that bring about significant positive change in individual, social, or environmental contexts.

Transformative Design goes beyond traditional design practices by placing a strong emphasis on empathy, collaboration, and human-centered approaches. It involves deeply understanding the needs, desires, and aspirations of the people who will be affected by the design, and using this understanding as a foundation for generating ideas and solutions.

The key principle of Transformative Design is the belief that design has the power to not only address specific problems or challenges, but also to spark larger transformations. It aims to create solutions that not only solve immediate issues, but also create long-term systemic change. This can involve challenging and redefining existing assumptions, structures, and processes, and designing alternative approaches that have the potential to disrupt and reshape existing systems.

Transformative Design is not limited to any particular discipline or field; it can be applied in areas such as product design, service design, social innovation, and environmental design. It requires interdisciplinary collaboration and a holistic understanding of complex challenges. By combining analytical thinking, creative problem-solving, and a deep understanding of human needs and aspirations, Transformative Design has the potential to create truly transformative and sustainable solutions.

Transition Planning

Transition planning in the context of Design Thinking disciplines refers to the process of preparing for the implementation of design solutions or changes within an organization or system. It involves strategically mapping out the steps and actions required to smoothly transition from the current state to the desired future state.

Design Thinking, as a problem-solving approach, emphasizes the need for thorough planning and preparation before executing any design solutions. Transition planning is an essential component of this approach as it ensures that the proposed design solutions are effectively implemented and integrated into the existing system or organization.

Transition Strategies

Transition strategies in the context of Design Thinking disciplines refer to the approaches and methods used to smoothly shift from one stage or phase of the design process to another. These strategies are aimed at ensuring a seamless transition that facilitates efficient and effective progression throughout the design thinking journey.

Transition strategies encompass a range of techniques and tools that help designers and teams navigate the various transitions within the design process. They involve managing the handoffs between different stages, activities, or team members, while maintaining clarity, focus, and momentum. These strategies can be applied at both micro and macro levels, addressing the transitions within individual tasks or activities, as well as the transitions between broader phases of the design process.

One common transition strategy is the use of clear communication and documentation. This involves effectively communicating project objectives, requirements, and progress updates to ensure that all stakeholders are on the same page. Additionally, documenting the findings, insights, and decisions made at each stage helps ensure continuity and enables informed decision-making in subsequent phases.

Another important transition strategy involves fostering a culture of collaboration and reflection. This includes encouraging open and transparent communication within the design team, as well as involving stakeholders and users throughout the process. By incorporating feedback and insights from various perspectives, designers can better navigate transitions and adapt their approach as needed.

Transparency

Transparency is a core principle in Agile Process and Project Management disciplines. It refers to the act of making information, decisions, and progress visible and easily accessible to all stakeholders involved in a project.

Transparency is crucial in Agile because it fosters trust, collaboration, and accountability among team members. By being transparent, project managers ensure that everyone is on the same page and has a clear understanding of the project goals, progress, and challenges.

In Agile, transparency is achieved through various practices and tools. Daily stand-up meetings, for example, provide a platform for team members to share updates, blockers, and next steps, allowing everyone to have visibility into each other's work. Additionally, visual management tools like Kanban boards or task boards enable teams to track progress, identify bottlenecks, and ensure work is flowing smoothly.

Transparency also extends to decision-making processes. Agile teams involve stakeholders and encourage an open and collaborative approach to decision making. This ensures that decisions are made collectively, considering different perspectives and expertise, and that all stakeholders have a shared understanding of the rationale behind them.

Overall, transparency in Agile Process and Project Management ensures that information flows freely, empowering teams to make informed decisions and adapt quickly to changes. By keeping everyone involved and informed, transparency increases the likelihood of project success.

Transparent Communication

Transparent communication is a key principle and practice within the discipline of Design Thinking. It refers to the open and honest exchange of information and ideas between all stakeholders involved in a design process.

Transparent communication fosters a collaborative and inclusive environment where diverse perspectives can be shared and understood. It encourages active listening, empathy, and trust among team members and stakeholders.

Usability Testing Platforms

Usability testing platforms are tools or software solutions that are used in the context of Design Thinking disciplines to evaluate the usability of a product, service, or user interface. These platforms provide a structured and controlled environment where researchers or designers can observe and gather feedback from users who interact with the design.

Through usability testing platforms, designers can identify potential usability issues, understand how users navigate through a product or interface, and gain insights on how to improve the overall user experience. These platforms typically offer features such as task scenarios, survey tools, screen capture and recording, and analytics to aid in the evaluation process.

Usability

Usability, in the context of Design Thinking disciplines, refers to the measure of how easily and efficiently a user can interact with a product, system, or service to achieve their desired goals.

It encompasses several factors, including learnability, efficiency, satisfaction, and flexibility. Learnability relates to how quickly users can understand and become proficient in using the product. Efficiency focuses on how effectively users can perform tasks once they have learned how to use the product. Satisfaction pertains to users' overall experience and emotional response when using the product. Lastly, flexibility considers the range of user preferences and needs that the product can accommodate.

User Acceptance Testing (UAT)

User Acceptance Testing (UAT) is a critical phase within the Agile Process and Project Management disciplines. It involves evaluating a software application or system's functionality, usability, and overall performance to ensure it meets the end user's requirements and expectations. UAT is conducted by the intended users or client representatives to validate the system's compliance with the specified business needs and to gain confidence in its effectiveness. During UAT, specific test cases are executed to ascertain the application's suitability for everyday use in real-world scenarios. This process involves identifying any defects, errors, or deviations from the desired outcome, and providing feedback for improvement. UAT is based on predefined acceptance criteria and clearly defined user stories, which reflect the target client's requirements and objectives. As part of the Agile Process, UAT tasks are usually performed in short iterations or sprints to validate incremental development efforts. It fosters collaboration and communication between developers, testers, and end users, promoting a collective understanding of the system's fitness for purpose. This iterative and collaborative approach allows for early detection and rectification of any potential issues, reducing the risk of late-stage failures or expensive rework. Through UAT, Agile practitioners can assess the software's compliance with user expectations and business objectives, ensuring the delivered product aligns with stakeholders' needs. It serves as a final gatekeeping mechanism, affirming the project's success and enabling stakeholders to make informed decisions regarding the acceptance or rejection of the system. In summary, UAT is a fundamental aspect of Agile Project Management, involving the end users in the testing process to validate the software against specified business needs. It facilitates collaboration, detects potential issues early on, and ensures the final product meets user expectations and objectives.

User Empowerment Workshops

User Empowerment Workshops refer to structured interactive sessions designed to provide individuals with the skills, knowledge, and tools necessary to take charge of their own experiences, decisions, and actions in a given domain or discipline. In the context of Design Thinking disciplines, these workshops aim to enable participants to become active and engaged contributors in the design process by fostering a sense of ownership, confidence, and agency.

During User Empowerment Workshops, participants have the opportunity to learn, practice, and apply various Design Thinking methods and techniques. They are encouraged to adopt a user-centered mindset and empathize with the end-users or stakeholders they are designing for. Through hands-on activities and collaborative exercises, participants develop a deep understanding of user needs, pain points, and aspirations. They also learn how to generate and evaluate innovative ideas, prototype and test solutions, and iterate based on user feedback.

User Experience (UX)

User Experience (UX) is a key component in the Design Thinking disciplines. It refers to the overall perception and satisfaction that users have while interacting with a product or service. This perception encompasses various aspects, including the ease of use, efficiency, and effectiveness of the product or service.

UX design involves understanding the user's needs, preferences, and goals in order to create a seamless and enjoyable experience. It encompasses the process of researching, designing, testing, and iterating to meet user expectations and enhance their satisfaction.

User Feedback

The Agile Process is a project management approach that emphasizes flexibility, collaboration, and iterative development. It involves breaking down a project into smaller, manageable tasks that can be completed in short timeframes called "sprints." The team works closely together, often in daily meetings, to discuss progress, address challenges, and make adjustments as needed.

Agile Project Management is a discipline focused on guiding and supporting teams in implementing Agile principles and practices. It provides tools and techniques for planning, organizing, and monitoring projects in an Agile environment. This discipline emphasizes the importance of clear communication, adaptability, and continuous improvement.

User Persona

User Persona is a fictional representation of the target audience that is created to better understand their characteristics, needs, and behaviors. It is widely used in Agile Process and Project Management disciplines to ensure that the development team has a clear understanding of who they are building the product for.

Creating a user persona helps the team to empathize with the end users and make informed decisions throughout the development process. A persona typically includes details such as demographic information, goals, motivations, and pain points of the target audience. By having a clear picture of the user persona, the team can align their efforts to meet the specific needs and expectations of that user.

User Stories

User stories are succinct, informal descriptions of a feature or requirement from the perspective of an end user. They are an essential tool in Design Thinking disciplines as they help teams empathize with the users, define their needs and desires, and come up with innovative solutions.

User stories consist of three parts: the role, the goal, and the benefit. The role represents the user or persona for whom the feature is being designed. It provides context and helps the team understand who they are designing for. The goal describes what the user wants to achieve or the problem they want to solve. It defines the purpose of the feature and ensures that it aligns with the user's needs. The benefit outlines the value that the user will gain from the feature. It highlights the positive impact it will have on their life or work.

User stories are usually expressed in a simple, non-technical language to ensure that they can be easily understood by all stakeholders. They are often written on index cards or sticky notes and displayed on a wall or whiteboard. This visual representation helps the team see the big picture and encourages collaboration and discussion.

By using user stories, Design Thinking teams can maintain a user-centric focus throughout the design and development process. They provide a clear and concise description of what needs to be done without getting caught up in technical details. User stories also facilitate communication and collaboration among team members, allowing for a more iterative and incremental approach to problem-solving.

User Story

User story is a technique in Agile Process and Project Management disciplines that captures the desired functionality or behavior of a software system from the perspective of its end users and stakeholders. It is a concise, informal statement written in the user's own words, focusing on what they need to accomplish or what problem they want to solve. Each user story typically follows a simple template: "As a [type of user], I want [some goal], so that [some reason]".

The user story serves as a placeholder for a conversation between the development team and the users or stakeholders. It acts as a reminder of the system's purpose and helps prioritize work by identifying the most valuable features or improvements. User stories also foster collaboration and promote understanding between team members, as they encourage discussions to clarify requirements and ensure a shared vision.

Unlike traditional requirements documentation, user stories are intentionally kept brief and flexible, avoiding excessive details and technical jargon. They are often written on index cards or post-it notes, making them easy to manage and rearrange. User stories are typically organized and prioritized in a backlog, which is a dynamic and evolving list of items that represent the work to be done. During backlog refinement or sprint planning, user stories may be further broken down into smaller, more manageable tasks.

Overall, user stories are a fundamental building block of Agile development, as they enable teams to prioritize and deliver software features incrementally, based on the needs and priorities of the users. Additionally, user stories promote a customer-centric and iterative approach to software development, where the focus is on delivering value quickly and continuously improving the product based on feedback.

User Testing Software

User testing software is a tool used in the context of Design Thinking disciplines to gather feedback and insights from users about a product or service. It enables designers and researchers to evaluate the usability, functionality, and overall user experience of a digital interface or physical product.

With user testing software, designers can create tasks and scenarios that simulate real-life situations and observe how users interact with the product. They can study user behavior, understand pain points, and identify areas of improvement. By capturing user actions, feedback, and emotions during the testing process, designers can make informed design decisions and refine their prototypes.

User Testing

Design thinking is a methodology used to understand and solve complex problems through a human-centered approach. It involves a set of principles and processes that encourage collaboration, creativity, and empathy in order to generate innovative solutions.

Design thinking is characterized by a deep understanding of the end-user or customer, with an emphasis on their needs, desires, and behaviors. This approach places the user at the center of the design process, with the goal of creating products, services, or experiences that truly meet their needs and provide value.

User-Centered Approach

A user-centered approach, within the context of Design Thinking disciplines, refers to a design methodology that focuses on understanding the needs, goals, and behaviors of the users or customers in order to create products or services that meet their specific requirements and preferences.

In this approach, designers engage in extensive research to gain insights into the target users, their context, and their pain points. This research involves various qualitative methods such as interviews, observations, and user testing to gather data and uncover patterns and trends. By empathizing with the users, designers try to understand their motivations, aspirations, and challenges, thus enabling them to develop effective and meaningful solutions.

Based on the information gathered, designers ideate, prototype, and test their ideas iteratively. They involve users at every stage of the design process, seeking feedback and validation. This collaborative approach ensures that user perspectives are integrated into the design solution, resulting in products that are truly user-centric.

A user-centered approach brings several advantages to the design process. By understanding users deeply, designers can uncover unmet needs and identify opportunities for innovation. It reduces the risk of creating products or services that fail to meet user expectations, as constant user feedback guides the design decisions. Ultimately, a user-centered approach enhances user satisfaction, increases usability, and fosters engagement, leading to the creation of products that truly address user needs and provide meaningful experiences.

User-Centered Approaches

User-centered approaches refer to design thinking disciplines that prioritize the needs, preferences, and experiences of the end users throughout the design process. The goal is to create products, services, or systems that are intuitive, effective, and enjoyable for the intended audience. By placing the user at the center of the design process, user-centered approaches aim to understand their behaviors, motivations, and pain points to inform the development of solutions that meet their needs. User-centered design is a cyclical process that involves multiple stages, beginning with empathizing with and understanding the users. This stage involves conducting research, interviews, and observations to gain insights into their goals, challenges, and context. The next stage is defining the problem or opportunity based on the user research findings. This helps to establish a clear design challenge that focuses on meeting the users' needs and solving their pain points. Ideation follows, where a range of possible solutions are generated. This is an opportunity for teams to brainstorm, explore different concepts, and engage in ideation exercises to foster creativity and divergent thinking. The best ideas are then selected and prototyped in the next stage. Prototypes can take various forms, such as low-fidelity sketches, mock-ups, or even interactive digital prototypes. Once prototypes are created, they are tested with users in order to gather feedback and insights. This feedback is crucial for refining the design and ensuring it aligns with the users' needs and expectations. This iterative feedback loop continues until a final design solution is reached. Overall, user-centered approaches acknowledge the value of involving the end users in the development process to create relevant, usable, and meaningful designs. By understanding the users' context, goals, and preferences, design solutions can be optimized to enhance the user experience and ultimately achieve greater product success.

User-Centered Collaboration Tools

User-Centered Collaboration Tools, within the context of Design Thinking disciplines, refer to digital platforms or software applications that are specifically designed to facilitate and enhance the collaborative process between team members, stakeholders, and end-users, with a strong focus on user needs and expectations. These tools enable the effective and efficient sharing of ideas, information, and feedback, fostering a dynamic and iterative approach to problem-solving. Such tools are typically characterized by their ability to support real-time communication and collaboration, allowing team members to work together synchronously or asynchronously, regardless of their location. They often provide features such as chat functionalities, video conferencing, document sharing, and version control, ensuring seamless interaction and integration of diverse perspectives throughout the design process. In the context of Design Thinking, which emphasizes a human-centric approach to problem-solving and innovation, user-centered collaboration tools hold immense value. They streamline the collaboration process between multidisciplinary teams, enabling them to better understand and empathize with the users they aim to serve. By providing a platform for effective communication and exchange of ideas, these tools facilitate the co-creation of solutions that truly address user needs and desires. Moreover, user-centered collaboration tools support the iterative nature of Design Thinking by enabling continuous feedback and refinement. They help teams collect and analyze user insights and observations in real-time, allowing for rapid prototyping and testing of ideas. This collaborative and iterative approach ultimately leads to the development of more user-friendly and impactful design solutions. In summary, user-centered collaboration tools are essential components of Design Thinking disciplines, as they empower teams to collaborate effectively, share knowledge, and build empathy with end-users. These tools facilitate the iterative process of design, ensuring that the final solutions are rooted in user needs and expectations.

User-Centered Education

User-Centered Education is an approach to teaching and learning that prioritizes the needs, perspectives, and experiences of students. Rooted in the principles of Design Thinking, this educational philosophy emphasizes empathy, collaboration, and iteration to create meaningful and effective learning experiences. In User-Centered Education, the learner is at the center of the educational process. Educators strive to understand the unique characteristics, interests, and goals of each student, employing a range of research methods such as observations, interviews, and surveys. This user research allows educators to gain insights into the students' motivations, challenges, and learning styles. Using the insights gathered from user research, educators then design and implement learning experiences that are tailored to meet the specific needs of their students. Rather than relying on a one-size-fits-all approach, User-Centered Education encourages customization and personalization. This may involve offering a variety of learning activities, providing options for student choice and autonomy, and adapting teaching techniques to match individual learning preferences. Throughout the learning process, User-Centered Education places a strong emphasis on collaboration and feedback. Students are encouraged to work together, share ideas, and build upon each other's knowledge and perspectives. Educators foster a culture of open communication, where students feel comfortable expressing their thoughts, asking questions, and giving and receiving constructive criticism. This collaborative environment helps to create a sense of community and promotes the development of vital social and emotional skills. User-Centered Education also embraces an iterative approach, acknowledging that learning is a dynamic and ongoing process. Both students and educators are encouraged to embrace failure as an opportunity for growth and to continuously reflect, revise, and refine their understanding and practices. This iterative process supports the development of critical thinking, adaptability, and resilience in both the learners and educators. Overall, User-Centered Education seeks to create a learning environment that is engaging, inclusive, and meaningful for all students. By placing the learner at the center and leveraging the principles of Design Thinking, this educational approach aims to empower students as active participants in their own education, equipping them with the knowledge, skills, and mindset necessary for success in an ever-evolving world.

User-Centered Evaluation

User-Centered Evaluation refers to the systematic assessment of a product or service from the perspective of the target users, with the aim of understanding their needs, goals, and preferences. It is a crucial step in the Design Thinking process, helping designers and stakeholders gain valuable insights into how well a design meets user requirements and expectations.

During the evaluation, various methods are employed to gather data and insights, such as user testing, surveys, interviews, and observation. These methods allow designers to assess the usability, functionality, and overall user experience of a product or service. By involving users in the evaluation process, designers can obtain real-world feedback and identify areas for improvement.

User-Centered Gamification

User-centered gamification is a strategic design approach that combines elements of game design with user-centered design principles to enhance user engagement, motivation, and behavior change in non-game contexts, such as websites, apps, or software. This approach aims to leverage the inherent motivational aspects of games, such as rewards, challenges, and progression, to create meaningful and enjoyable user experiences. In the context of Design Thinking disciplines, user-centered gamification involves understanding the needs, goals, and motivations of the target users through user research and empathy. This information is then used to design game mechanics that are aligned with the users' desired outcomes and preferences. These game mechanics can include points, badges, leaderboards, levels, and social interactions, among others. The key principle of user-centered gamification is to make the experience enjoyable and rewarding for the users, while also aligning with the desired goals of the organization or project. It is important to design game elements that provide a sense of autonomy, competence, and relatedness to the users, as these factors have been shown to enhance motivation and engagement. By implementing user-centered gamification, organizations can create more engaging and motivating experiences for their users, which can lead to increased user adoption, retention, and satisfaction. It can also drive behavior change and support the achievement of desired outcomes, such as learning, wellness, or productivity. Overall, user-centered gamification is a powerful design approach that can be used to enhance user experiences and drive behavior change in various non-game contexts.

User-Centric

User-Centric refers to a customer-focused approach in Agile Process and Project Management disciplines. It emphasizes the importance of understanding the needs and expectations of the end users and designing solutions that meet those needs effectively. In User-Centric Agile practices, user feedback and collaboration play a crucial role in driving the development process. In Agile Process Management, user-centricity is achieved through continuous user involvement and feedback. User stories and personas are used to represent the different types of users and their specific needs, helping the development team to align their efforts towards creating value for the end users. By actively involving users in the process, the team gains a better understanding of their preferences, pain points, and desired functionalities, which can be prioritized and incorporated into the product backlog. User-Centric Project Management in an Agile context requires the project team to put the end user at the center of their decision-making process. It involves actively seeking user feedback through methods like user testing sessions, surveys, and interviews. The insights gained from this feedback are then used to inform and guide the development process. User-Centric Project Management also involves regular communication and collaboration with stakeholders to ensure that the project goals align with the expectations and needs of the end users. Overall, User-Centric Agile Process and Project Management disciplines ensure that the development efforts are focused on delivering value to the end users. Incorporating user feedback and involving them in the decision-making process leads to improved user satisfaction, higher adoption rates, and a more successful project outcome.

Value Chain

The value chain in the context of Agile Process and Project Management disciplines refers to a series of activities and processes that organizations undertake to deliver value to customers. It encompasses the entire lifecycle of a project, from the initial planning and requirements gathering phase to the final delivery and support phase.

In Agile Process and Project Management, the value chain is often characterized by frequent iterations and continuous feedback loops. It focuses on delivering valuable increments of work to customers at regular intervals, allowing for quick adaptation and change.

Value Co-Creation Workshops

Value Co-Creation Workshops are collaborative sessions within the framework of Design Thinking disciplines, which aim to engage all stakeholders involved in the creation and delivery of a product or service. These workshops provide a structured environment for participants to come together and collectively generate ideas, insights, and solutions to address a specific problem or challenge.

During these workshops, diverse perspectives and expertise are brought together to foster creativity, innovation, and empathy. The focus is not only on solving the problem at hand but also on ensuring that the solutions created are valuable to the end-users and stakeholders. The process encourages active participation, encourages dialogue and ideation, and promotes a culture of collaboration and co-creation.

Value Co-Creation

Value co-creation, in the context of design thinking disciplines, refers to the collaborative process of creating value by involving various stakeholders in the design and development of a product, service, or experience. It is based on the principle that value is not solely determined by the provider but is co-created through interactions and contributions from both the provider and the customer or end-user.

In value co-creation, designers, users, and other relevant stakeholders actively engage in a participatory design approach to understand and address users' needs, desires, and aspirations. This approach goes beyond the traditional notion of customers as passive recipients of products and services and recognizes their active role in shaping and enhancing the value proposition.

Value Proposition

The value proposition in the context of Design Thinking disciplines refers to the unique combination of benefits and advantages that a design solution offers to its users or customers. It is a statement that articulates the value that a product, service, or design concept brings to its target audience.

A well-defined value proposition addresses the needs, desires, and pain points of the users and clearly highlights how the design solution solves their problems or fulfills their desires better than any alternative. It helps in creating a strong differentiation and competitive advantage for the product or service in the market.

Value Stream Mapping

Value Stream Mapping (VSM) is a visual tool used in Agile Process and Project Management disciplines to analyze and improve the flow of value from the customer's perspective. It provides a comprehensive overview of the entire process involved in delivering a product or service, highlighting the current state and identifying areas of improvement.

VSM involves mapping out each step in the value stream, including both value-added and non-value-added activities, as well as information flows and decision points. This mapping allows teams to identify bottlenecks, waste, and areas of inefficiency in the process, enabling them to streamline operations and increase productivity.

Value Stream

A value stream in the context of Agile Process and Project Management disciplines refers to the end-to-end flow of activities and processes that deliver value to customers. It encompasses all the steps and resources involved in creating and delivering a product or service, from the initial concept to the final delivery.

The value stream is visualized as a series of interconnected steps, with each step representing a specific task or process. These steps are organized in a logical sequence, with outputs from one step becoming inputs for the next. The goal of value stream mapping is to understand and optimize the flow of value through the entire system, identifying areas of waste and opportunities for improvement.

By mapping the value stream, Agile teams and project managers gain insights into the overall process, enabling them to identify bottlenecks, streamline workflows, and eliminate non-value-added activities. This allows for faster delivery of customer value, improved quality, and increased productivity.

The value stream approach is distinct in its focus on value as perceived by the customer. It aligns with Agile principles of delivering the highest value features early and continuously, while avoiding unnecessary work or rework. Value stream mapping is often used in Agile frameworks, such as Scrum or Kanban, to identify and prioritize user stories or tasks based on customer value and to optimize the flow of work through the team.

Value-Based Prioritization

Value-Based Prioritization is a technique used in Agile Process and Project Management disciplines to determine the order in which work should be completed based on the estimated value it will bring to the project or organization. It involves assessing and ranking the potential benefits of each work item or task against its cost or effort.

In Agile methodologies like Scrum, where project requirements can evolve throughout the process, value-based prioritization helps the team make informed decisions about what work to pursue next. By constantly evaluating and re-prioritizing the backlog of tasks, the team can maximize the value delivered to the customer or business.

Value-Driven Development

Value-driven development is a concept within the Agile process and project management disciplines that focuses on delivering maximum value to stakeholders. It emphasizes collaboration, adaptability, and continuous improvement to effectively meet customer needs and expectations.

At its core, value-driven development is centered around the agile principle of delivering working software frequently and consistently, with a strong focus on customer satisfaction. It entails a holistic approach that encompasses multiple aspects, including requirements analysis, iterative development, and regular customer feedback.

Value-driven development places a high importance on prioritizing requirements based on their business value, ensuring that features with the greatest impact on customer value are delivered first. This approach allows for the early identification and integration of valuable features, while also facilitating quick responsiveness to changing customer needs.

Additionally, value-driven development emphasizes the importance of close collaboration between the development team and stakeholders. Regular communication and feedback loops enable continuous improvement and help ensure that the developed software is aligned with the evolving priorities of the project.

Overall, value-driven development empowers teams to optimize the value of their deliverables by adaptively responding to customer needs and focusing on high-priority features. By embracing flexibility, collaboration, and continuous improvement, it enables organizations to maximize customer satisfaction and successfully navigate the complexities of Agile project management.

Value

Value, in the context of Agile Process and Project Management disciplines, refers to the worth or benefit that a particular deliverable or feature provides to the customer or end user. It is a fundamental concept in Agile methodologies, which prioritize delivering high-value items to the customer early and frequently.

Agile processes focus on delivering value by breaking down projects into small increments called iterations or sprints. Each iteration aims to produce a working product that provides value to the customer. By working closely with the customer and regularly gathering feedback, Agile teams can ensure that the delivered product meets the customer's needs and provides the desired value.

Variance

Variance is defined as the measurement of the deviation or difference between planned and actual project performance. In the context of Agile Process and Project Management disciplines, variance plays a crucial role in monitoring and controlling project progress.

In Agile, projects are developed incrementally and iteratively, with continuous feedback and adaptation. This iterative nature allows for early detection of variances and enables timely corrective actions, ensuring the project remains on track. Variance analysis provides insights into project deviations from the original plan, helping Agile teams identify potential risks and take proactive measures to address them.

Velocity

Velocity is a metric used in Agile Process and Project Management disciplines to measure the rate at which a team delivers value. It refers to the amount of work completed by the team within a specific timeframe, typically measured in iterations or sprints.

Velocity is calculated by summing up the story points or work items completed by the team during a sprint or iteration. It provides insights into the team's productivity, efficiency, and capacity to deliver value to the customer.

Virtual Reality Prototyping

Virtual reality prototyping is a method used in the field of design thinking to create immersive virtual experiences with the aim of exploring, evaluating, and refining design concepts. It involves the use of digital tools and technologies to simulate and visualize potential solutions before they are implemented in the physical world.

By leveraging virtual reality technology, designers can develop interactive and three-dimensional prototypes that allow users to navigate and interact with the design in a realistic and immersive way. This enables designers to gain valuable insights into the user experience and identify potential design flaws early in the development process.

Virtual Whiteboarding Tools

Virtual whiteboarding tools are digital platforms or applications that allow users to collaborate and ideate in a creative and visual manner. These tools aim to replicate the traditional whiteboard experience in a virtual environment, enabling individuals or teams to brainstorm, plan, and organize their ideas.

Specifically in the context of Design Thinking disciplines, virtual whiteboarding tools facilitate the various stages of the design process, from problem identification to solution development. These tools provide a space where team members can collectively generate ideas, visually map out concepts, and evaluate potential solutions.

Visual Management

Visual Management in the context of Agile Process and Project Management disciplines refers to the practice of using visual aids and tools to enhance communication, collaboration, and understanding within Agile teams. It involves the use of visual cues, such as charts, boards, and diagrams, to convey information, progress, and status in a clear and transparent manner.

Visual Management plays a crucial role in Agile project management as it enables teams to visualize their work, track progress, identify bottlenecks, and make informed decisions. By using visual representations, such as Kanban boards, burndown charts, and task boards, teams can easily grasp the current state of the project and identify areas that require attention or improvement.

Visual Management promotes transparency and clarity by providing a common visual language that enables team members to understand and discuss project-related information easily. It encourages collaboration and fosters a shared understanding of the project's goals, priorities, and progress among all team members.

By utilizing visual aids, teams can quickly identify dependencies, visualize work in progress, and optimize workflow. This allows for effective resource allocation, efficient task management, and timely delivery of project milestones.

In summary, Visual Management in Agile Process and Project Management disciplines is the practice of using visual aids and tools to enhance communication, collaboration, and understanding within Agile teams. It promotes transparency, clarity, and shared understanding of project-related information, enabling teams to make informed decisions and deliver value in a timely manner.

WIP (Work In Progress) Limit

A Work in Progress (WIP) Limit is a technique used in Agile Process and Project Management disciplines to enhance productivity and reduce bottlenecks in project workflows by placing restrictions on the amount of work that can be in progress at any given time.

The WIP Limit is set in order to optimize the flow of work through the system, preventing overburdening of team members and ensuring a smooth and efficient progression of tasks throughout the project. It sets a maximum threshold for how many tasks or user stories can be actively worked on simultaneously, encouraging teams to focus on completing existing work before taking on new tasks.

Implementing a WIP Limit helps in visualizing and minimizing work-in-progress, which in turn reduces multitasking, improves team communication and collaboration, and increases overall efficiency. By limiting the number of active tasks, teams are able to identify bottlenecks and address them promptly, leading to faster completion of work and shorter lead times.

This technique aligns with Agile principles such as continuous delivery and promotes a more sustainable pace of work for team members. It encourages the prioritization and completion of tasks rather than accumulating a backlog of partially completed work. By streamlining the flow of work, teams can better manage their resources, optimize throughput, and deliver high-quality outcomes in a timely manner.

WIP (Work In Progress)

WIP, also known as Work in Progress, is a term commonly used in Agile Process and Project Management disciplines. It refers to the tasks or activities that are currently being worked on but have not yet been completed or delivered. In Agile methodologies, such as Scrum, WIP is a crucial concept that helps teams manage their work effectively and ensure a smooth workflow.

WIP can be seen as a snapshot of the work items that are currently in motion. These could be user stories, features, or any other unit of work that has been started but not yet finished. It represents the ongoing effort and resources dedicated to accomplishing these tasks. By tracking WIP, teams can have visibility into the amount of work in progress and easily identify any bottlenecks or issues that might arise during the project.

Managing WIP is essential in Agile project management as it allows teams to optimize their workflow and maintain a sustainable pace of work. Limiting the amount of work in progress helps prevent overloading team members and ensures that focus and attention are given to completing tasks rather than starting new ones.

By setting explicit limits on WIP, teams can improve their efficiency and reduce the time it takes to complete work items. This helps in achieving a higher level of productivity and increases the predictability of project delivery. WIP limits also encourage collaboration and promote a culture of finishing what has been started before moving on to new tasks.

Waste Reduction

Waste reduction in the context of Agile Process and Project Management refers to the practice of minimizing or eliminating any activities, processes, or resources that do not add value to the project or product. It is aimed at increasing efficiency, optimizing productivity, and improving overall project outcomes.

Agile methodologies, such as Scrum or Kanban, emphasize the importance of waste reduction by promoting continuous improvement and prioritizing value-centric activities. Waste can manifest in various forms within an Agile project, including but not limited to:

1. Task-switching: Unnecessary switches between different tasks or priorities, resulting in lost time and reduced productivity.

2. Overproduction: Generating excess documentation, features, or deliverables that are not required or valued by the stakeholders.

3. Waiting time: Idle periods where team members are waiting for dependencies, feedback, or approvals, leading to delays and inefficiencies.

4. Defects and rework: Errors or defects in the deliverables that require additional effort and resources to fix and retest.

5. Excess inventory: Accumulation of unfinished work or work in progress, leading to longer lead times and increased risk of obsolescence.

By identifying and minimizing these forms of waste, Agile teams can focus on value-added activities, deliver high-quality outputs, and maintain a sustainable pace of work. Waste reduction is a continuous process that requires regular reflection, collaboration, and adaptation to ensure optimal project and product outcomes in an Agile environment.

Waste

Waste refers to any activity or process that does not add value and can be eliminated or minimized without affecting the overall outcome of a project, as per the principles of Agile Process and Project Management disciplines.

In Agile, waste is identified as anything that does not contribute to the creation of a high-quality end product or accelerate the delivery of value to the customer. Agile methodologies prioritize efficiency, continuous improvement, and the elimination of non-essential work, aiming to streamline the development process and optimize resource utilization.

There are several types of waste that Agile teams seek to mitigate:

1. Overproduction: Producing more than what is required or requested by the customer, leading to excess inventory or unused features.

2. Waiting: Delays caused by waiting for approvals, feedback, or dependencies to be resolved, resulting in idle time and decreased productivity.

3. Transportation: Excessive movement of information, materials, or code between individuals or departments, introducing additional risk and opportunities for errors.

4. Defects: Errors or defects in the software or product that require rework or debugging, affecting both time and quality.

5. Overprocessing: Performing unnecessary or redundant steps in a process, consuming resources without adding value.

6. Motion: Unnecessary movement or activities within the workspace that do not contribute to the completion of tasks.

7. Inventory: Accumulation of excess work-in-progress items, leading to increased lead times and decreased flexibility.

By identifying and reducing these forms of waste, Agile teams can optimize their processes, increase efficiency, and enhance customer satisfaction by delivering value more effectively.

Waterfall

The waterfall methodology is a linear, sequential approach to project management that consists of distinct phases, with each phase dependent on the completion of the previous one. It is commonly used in traditional project management practices and is considered to be the opposite of agile methodologies.

In the waterfall methodology, the project is divided into sequential stages, such as requirements gathering, design, development, testing, and deployment. These stages are performed in a linear fashion, meaning that they must be completed before moving on to the next stage. Each stage has its own set of deliverables and milestones, and once a stage is completed, it is often difficult to make changes or go back to a previous stage.

Work In Progress (WIP) Limit

A Work in Progress (WIP) limit is a constraint imposed on the number of unfinished items or tasks that can be in progress simultaneously within an Agile process or project management discipline. It is used to optimize workflow and ensure that teams focus on completing work rather than starting new tasks indefinitely.

The purpose of implementing a WIP limit is to reduce multitasking, minimize context switching, and improve overall productivity. By setting a maximum threshold for work in progress, teams can prevent bottlenecks, increase visibility, and maintain a steady flow of completed work.

Workshop Facilitation

Workshop facilitation, in the context of Design Thinking disciplines, refers to the process of guiding a group of individuals through a collaborative workshop session. The facilitator plays a crucial role in creating an environment that fosters creativity, open communication, and effective problem-solving.

During a workshop, the facilitator employs various techniques and methods to encourage active participation from all participants, ensuring that every voice is heard. They may use brainstorming sessions, group activities, and icebreaker exercises to break down barriers and encourage collaboration among diverse perspectives.

XP (Extreme Programming)

Extreme Programming (XP) is an Agile software development methodology that emphasizes teamwork, collaboration, and adaptability. It is a project management discipline that aims to deliver high-quality software in a constantly changing and unpredictable environment.

XP follows a set of core values, including simplicity, communication, feedback, and courage. It encourages frequent communication and collaboration between all members of the development team, including developers, testers, and customers. XP promotes a culture of open and honest communication to ensure that everyone is aligned and working towards the same goals.

In XP, software development is performed in short iterations, typically lasting one to three weeks. Each iteration focuses on delivering a small, working piece of software that provides business value. This allows for frequent feedback and enables the team to adapt quickly to changing requirements or priorities.

The XP development process consists of several practices, including test-driven development (TDD), pair programming, continuous integration, and collective code ownership. TDD involves writing automated tests before writing the actual code, which helps ensure that the software meets the specified requirements and remains maintainable over time. Pair programming promotes collaboration and knowledge sharing by having two developers work together on the same task.

XP also emphasizes continuous integration, which involves integrating and testing all changes to the codebase frequently. This reduces the risk of integration issues and allows for faster feedback on any defects or regressions. Collective code ownership means that all developers are responsible for the quality of the codebase and can make changes anywhere in the code to improve it.

www.ingramcontent.com/pod-product-compliance
Lightning Source LLC
LaVergne TN
LVHW092030060326
832903LV00058B/488